Charles Penrose Keith

The Ancestry of Benjamin Harrison

President of the United States of America, 1889-1893

Charles Penrose Keith

The Ancestry of Benjamin Harrison
President of the United States of America, 1889-1893

ISBN/EAN: 9783337126636

Printed in Europe, USA, Canada, Australia, Japan

Cover: Foto ©ninafisch / pixelio.de

More available books at **www.hansebooks.com**

THE ANCESTRY

OF

BENJAMIN HARRISON

PRESIDENT OF THE UNITED STATES OF AMERICA 1889-1893

IN CHART FORM SHOWING ALSO THE DESCENDANTS OF

WILLIAM HENRY HARRISON

PRESIDENT OF THE UNITED STATES OF AMERICA IN 1841

AND

Notes on Families Related

BY
CHARLES P. KEITH
AUTHOR OF "THE PROVINCIAL COUNCILLORS OF PENNSYLVANIA 1733-1776" ETC.

PHILADELPHIA
1893

INTRODUCTION.

The following work, for which the undersigned alone is responsible, it having proceeded neither from the suggestion, nor under the supervision, of any one else, is published for its merits as an attempt to show, not merely the paternal line, but all the other forefathers of an individual. The actual forefathers being arranged in a chart, data which have been found as to the collateral branches of some of the families are included, with the evidence for the direct lines, in this Introduction and the notes which follow it, headed by the various names, and an effort has been made to give an account, complete to date, of the Irwin and of the Ramsey family. It is not pretended that the pedigree adds to the distinction of a man who has been President of the United States of America. That office, to be sure, is neither the apex of a system of caste, like a European king's, nor the object of eighteen centuries' veneration, like the Pope's, nor the control of the lives and property of millions, like the Czar's or the ruler of China's; but, at the head of such a nation as ours has become, it is one of the very greatest positions on the earth. Its constitutional functions affect double the extent of territory that Charlemagne ruled. Surrounding the incumbent with no luxury, and rigidly subjecting him to law, it nevertheless resembles, with its unpretentious title, its actual power, its operation through a Senate, its preponderance in a hemisphere, that of the early Roman emperors, before the abrogation of republican forms. Few contemporary lives are as much studied as those culminating, or suggested to culminate, in the White House; and, as the ancestry of any man is a fact, important or otherwise, in his history, it is supposed that, while genealogists will value any work showing how far in each line, male and female, the ancestors of a living American can be traced, other people will be interested in such data concerning a President. The paternal line of the one whose term ended on the 4th of last March is unique from the standing anterior to the Revolutionary War, and the service during it and since. Moreover, while it is rare, in this young country, to find, even among the Presidents, any person all of whose great-grandfathers were Americans, he descends from many families known to have been here nearly two hundred years before his birth. This makes such a work relating to Benjamin Harrison a contribution to the genealogy of many of his fellow-citizens.

All the known ancestors who lived in America are mentioned in the chart. An effort has been made to trace back of this country nearly every surname thus introduced; and each has been carried as far as appeared certain, except that the Bedell pedigree, which can be found in the *Visitation of Huntingdonshire*, has not been transcribed. The ancestral lines met with through the wives of men who never came to America, have been followed where they seemed to lead to interesting personages; and, indeed, as we advance into ancient times, we can be positive of the genealogy of those only who were so conspicuous that theirs was of public notoriety. I have succeeded in working out the ancestry, with a fair amount of evidence for every step, further than any other American's has been extended, as far as I am aware. In so doing, however, I must not be charged with furnishing a basis for pride of birth. Nothing could be more democratic than genealogy carried far enough to point out the descent or kinship between the most exalted and the humblest. As the number of a man's ancestors back of a few centuries is enormous, having doubled with each generation, except where, being relatives, they had lines in common, some historical celebrities must be included. Three hundred years ago, no difference of caste separated the poorer gentry of England from the yeomanry and tradespeople; and five hundred years ago, the royal family intermarried with subjects as frequently as with foreign potentates. So a far-off king is likely to have descendants in all stations of life. There is nobody living except a Bourbon known to be a legitimate descendant of any king or emperor mentioned in this chart through males; but through females the blood of Clovis, of Charlemagne, and of Alfred must flow in the veins of vast numbers of people, while even that of the Conqueror or of the early Plantagenets is probably in so many that it cannot be claimed as distinguishing. We mean by legitimate descent. Starting with fifteen grandchildren of King Edward I., which fifteen are known to have married and left lawful issue, and allowing to each of them two children married and having lawful issue, and so on, assuming the number of such descendants to double in each generation, we obtain nearly 4,000,000 in the twentieth generation from the king. That this estimate is not too large, that, except when cut off by war, or narrowed by intermarriages, families spread more rapidly, there is an instance in the chart. The estimate would allow for four grandchildren of President William Henry Harrison having families: there are six times that many.

No line in this work is carried through any person whose birth appears to have been illegitimate. There is no suspicion of illegitimate birth as to any one mentioned in the work who lived in America, or in fact who was born since A.D. 1400. Where the legitimacy depends upon the validity of a marriage under peculiar circumstances, of which there are several cases in the older part, I have been controlled by the acquiescence or the decision of the contemporary ecclesiastical power, then the recognized arbiter of such matters. Thus the marriages of King Henry II. of England with the divorced Eleanor, and of the divorced Earl of Arundel with a daughter of the Earl of Lancaster, and of the divorced Lord Mowbray with another daughter of the Earl of Lancaster, have been treated as valid; but the parents of Louis IV., "d'Outremer," King of France, and of Ferdinand III., King of Castille, are not mentioned, because the marriages of the parents were not deemed lawful. But in popular language, and a layman's view, the only real bastards in the chart were Hameline Plantagenet, William the Conqueror, and Bernard, King of Italy, and possibly Charles Martel; and perhaps also the issue of Chilperic I., heathen King of the Franks, and the abducted wife of a king of Thuringia, said issue being Clovis, the first Christian King of the Franks, would be so considered.

Much of the American part of the chart will be found in either Bishop Meade's *Old Churches, Ministers, and Families of Virginia*, which is authority for so much family history as may be supposed to have lain within the knowledge of his contemporaries, or Savage's *Genealogical Dictionary of New England*, Vinton's *Symmes Memorial*, or Tuttle's *Descendants of William and Elizabeth Tuttle*. I have derived my knowledge of the records in Virginia other than parochial, and of the tombstone inscriptions not taken from Bishop Meade's work, made use of either in the chart or in the accounts of families following this Introduction, from the publications of the Virginia Historical Society, or articles in periodicals by, and correspondence with, Mrs. Ella Bassett Washington, Pres. Lyon G. Tyler, Alexander Brown, W. G. Stanard, R. A. Brock, and others. In that part of the chart which consists of a table of the descendants of President William Henry Harrison, I have made use of much data collected by Frank Willing Leach for his projected work on the descendants of the Signers of the Declaration of Independence.

In the absence of a contemporaneous statement, it is hard to discover and fix positively the parentage of a former emigrant, unless the date of his birth can be closely approximated, and he has left some memorandum of the parish in which he was born, and the records of that parish are accessible. Despite the contrary notion somewhat prevalent, very few of those who removed to Virginia, or any other part of North America, during the colonial period, figure in the peerage books or county histories of the British Isles; and the herald's visitations which have been published, are too far from complete, and, even with the continuations made by the copyists, are mostly too early to be of assistance. The notes following this Introduction will explain how the respective families have been traced back of this country. I will here give the authorities for the longest line. The Colonial grandee, born about the end of the year 1663, who has been called "King Carter," who named one of his children Ludlow, was, it is agreed, the son of John Carter and Sarah Ludlow, his wife. The tombstone over that couple and three other wives tells us that Sarah's father was "Mr. Gabriel Ludlow." There was a

Roger Ludlow, Deputy Governor of Massachusetts, and afterwards of Connecticut, and a George Ludlow, member of the Virginia Council, whose will, styling him of York County, was probated August 1, 1656. The celebrated Parliamentary General Ludlow speaks in his Memoirs of this kinsman's services to the Parliamentary side. George left most of his property to the children of his brother Roger, and the children of his brother Gabriel. The latter's daughter Sarah is mentioned in the will of Gabriel's widow dated September 20, 1657, which appears in Brown's *Abstracts of Somersetshire Wills*. Sarah's brother Thomas received his uncle's farm in York County, Virginia, and probably brought her to America. A pedigree of the Ludlow family has been prepared recently by Henry Hungerford Ludlow-Bruges of Seend, Melksham, England, a portion being reprinted in the *New England Historical and Genealogical Register*. It shows us that Roger, George, and Gabriel aforesaid were first cousins of General Ludlow's father, and were the sons of Thomas Ludlow of Dinton, and grandsons of George Ludlow of the old seat at Hill Deverill. The marriage of Edith, daughter of Lord Windsor, to George Ludlow of Hill Deverill is mentioned in terms of self-congratulation in Lord Windsor's will, dated in 1543, abstracted in Nicholas's *Testamenta Vetusta*. That this Edith was the mother of Thomas of Dinton is proved by family deeds, as well as by a herald's visitation made in 1565, in the lifetime of his father. The latter's ancestry as far as it is set forth in the chart also appears in this visitation. The memorandum of the wills, I have taken from the pedigree recently prepared. The ancestry of Lord Windsor's father-in-law, I have taken mainly from Sir Alexander Croke's *Genealogical History of the Croke Family, originally named Le Blount*. For so much of the Spanish pedigree as I have used, he appears to have had as authority the writings of the celebrated statesman and author, Don Pedro Lopez de Ayala, who was uncle of Sir Walter Blount's wife, and who speaks of her marriage with " un Cavellero de Inglaterra que dijeron Mossen Gauter Blont, del qual ovo fijos a Mossen Juan Blonte, un bueno Cavallero, qui murió en la cerca de Roa," etc. The *Cronicas de la Casa de Viscaya* in the British Museum, Egerton MS. 897, which I have consulted independently, corroborate the statement that Don Lope Diaz de Haro had as his third legitimate son Don Lope Ruys, whom it calls Don Rui Lopez.

In the rest of my work, I have not merely transcribed heralds' visitations, Dugdale's *Baronage of England*, Dugdale's own Addenda thereto (printed in *Collectanea Topographica. et Genealogica*), or Anderson's *Royal Genealogies*. I have weighed their authority, and tried to verify any statement requiring verification. As there had been for a long period prior to the settlement of America a body of officials who had the regulation of coats of arms, and whose business it was to know descents and relationships, it perhaps would be sufficient to cite documents prepared by them;

Introduction. 7

but I have not contented myself with this. I have sought better evidence, and have depended upon their statements only where they appear to be founded on charters or records of the time of which they speak, or the knowledge which living persons had of their nearest ancestors. The earliest of the heralds' visitations took place in the time of King Henry VIII.; but most of the genealogical notes of which I have made use were written about the year 1600. The earliest work on the peerage which I have consulted, although it is not the earliest extant, is *Baronagium Angliæ, A.D. 1587,* a manuscript in the British Museum. It is nearly contemporary with the first Lord Windsor, but does not give his ancestry: it mentions his wife, "Elizabetha soror et una heredum Edwardi Blont Dni de Montjoy." This manuscript and all others in England which I have consulted, except parish registers, but including wills and administrations, were examined and transcribed, or abstracts of them made, by Miss Emma M. Walford, 46 Great Coram Street, W. C., London. Of much value, as a guide at least, has been an elaborate tabular view of the ancestry of Lord Thomas Windsor, prepared evidently soon after March 30, 1610, found in Harleian codex 1195. It professes to give "The true and Anncyent descent of ye right Honorable Thomas Lord Windsor deduced ffrom ye Body of Sr. Walter Windsor a Norman and ffrom ye Conquest, as it was gathered out of ye Anncient records of that honorable ffamilye vnto this present yere," of which male line I have copied very little; but several maternal lines are also given, and such of these as blend in the children of Sir Andrews, first Lord Windsor, I have investigated.

The will of Sir Andrews Windsor's grandmother, Ellzabeth Andrews, and that of her "sister," step-sister, or sister-in-law, Alice Wyche, and that of Thomas Windsor, appear in *Testamenta Vetusta,* and verify the line as far as Mrs. Andrews, not disclosing, however, her parentage. Collins, in his *Peerage of England,* which seems to be the best work on that subject, gives her father.

Blomefield's *History of Norfolk* says that Augustine Stratton, Esq., and John Stratton, citizen and mercer of London (Augustine, I suppose, being John's father), purchased Tye Hall in 1416, that John Stratton was lord of Tye Hall, Lyons, and Aldenhams in Weston in the 8th year of Henry VI., when they were settled on John and his wife Elizabeth and their heirs, and that by said wife he had an only daughter, who married John Andrews, Esq., of Baylham, Suffolk, to whom and Elizabeth his wife, in the 8th of Edward IV., the manor of Weston was transferred. Blomefield, who may have reached the conclusion independently of the authorities which I have consulted, expresses the opinion that Stratton's wife Elizabeth was daughter of Andrew or Hugh Luttrell. Various genealogical manuscripts make her the daughter of Sir Andrew, notably the pedigree on f. 376 of No. 5524 of the Additional MSS. in the British Museum, of the date of the preparation of which I am ignorant. To a pedigree, in the same handwriting, of the Suliard family, Sir John Suliard, Chief Justice of the Common Pleas, having married the other daughter of John and Elizabeth Andrews, there has been added, in later handwriting, the latter's descent from the Luttrells, as follows: Elizabeth being daughter of "John Straiton of Weston in Suffolk" by "Elizabeth, dar. and heire" of "Huge Lutterell K." by "Katherin, dar. to John Beamont a. y. bary of 6." There is thus an agreement that Elizabeth Andrews's mother was daughter of a Luttrell. She was, indeed, the daughter of Sir Hugh, as the tabular view of Lord Thomas Windsor's ancestry declares, and H. C. Maxwell Lyte, C. B., now Deputy Keeper of the Public Records of England, has so stated in a pedigree of the Luttrell family prepared in 1882. He has communicated to me the proof that Sir Hugh had a daughter Elizabeth, which is found in a deed of the year 1406, preserved at Dunster Castle, settling upon her the manor of Debenham, she marrying William Harleston. That afterwards she married John Stratton, is stated in the inquisition in the 21st year of Edward IV. upon the death of her son William Harleston, which speaks of her as the daughter of Sir Hugh, and says that she had a daughter Elizabeth by John Stratton, and had departed this life. The notes on the Harleston family in additional MS. 19134 in the British Museum quote the genealogical collections of Norris to the effect that the elder William Harleston died in 1419, and his wife Elizabeth, da. of ——, afterwards married John Stratton of Suffolk, Esq., and was the latter's wife in 1439. By will dated 4 Kal. October, 1438, also quoted, Peter Maudby appointed as executors, Elizabeth, wife of John Stratton, and her son, William Harleston. An account of Elizabeth's father, Sir Hugh, and of her grandparents, Sir Andrew Luttrell and his wife Elizabeth, daughter of the Earl of Devon, is found in Collinson's *History and Antiquities of the County of Somerset*; and Blomefield's *History of Norfolk* has some further information. "Hugh Lutterell" is named in the will of Margaret, Countess of Devon, in 1391, as is also the testatrix's "daughter Lutterell:" see *Testamenta Vetusta*. The dates relating to the Princess Elizabeth in the chart have been taken from Green's *Lives of the Princesses of England*.

The tabular view of Lord Windsor's ancestors shows the connection given in the chart with the Echynghams. It is confirmed by a book on *the Echynghams of Echyngham* by Spencer Hall. This and an article on *Echingham Church* in the *Sussex Archæological Collections*, setting forth the monumental inscriptions and escutcheons, carry that family to Joanna, wife of Sir William. Although I have not undertaken to trace his progenitors, they had been of importance since the reign of King John. One of them, in Edward II's. reign, had been summoned as a baron to Parliament. A recent predecessor of Sir William had built the church referred to, which is still standing. So there was no such disparity between the lord of that manor and a grand-daughter of the House of Arundel as would make a matrimonial alliance between them unlikely. The statement made, not in the tabular view aforesaid, but in the works above mentioned, that Joanna was a daughter of John of Arundel, Lord Maltravers, is found in various genealogical manuscripts, particularly some notes on the family, prepared possibly near the year which is mentioned in one of the pedigrees, viz. 1596, included in the Collections relating to Sussex of the celebrated herald Augustus Vincent, which Collections are now in the College of Arms, in London. Perhaps a little earlier than this, viz., during the life apparently of a certain Edward Echingham of Bassam, claiming descent from this family, a pedigree was prepared, which is in Harleian MS. 1174 in the British Museum, making the same statement. It is perhaps the only pedigree in which the statement appears, which seems to have been gotten up to flatter anybody; yet it seems merely to give the known data about Edward's family, and about the older line, and to leave blank the connecting links. The earliest statement of this marriage of which I have knowledge, was in the writings consulted for "Genealogia familiae de Fitzalen Comitum Arundelle," on f. 11 of a volume of collections by the celebrated antiquary William Camden, written in his own hand, entitled "Miscellanea ex variis scriptoribus collecta, 1573," which is No. 229 of the Lansdowne MSS. in the British Museum. The date of the original writings is unknown, but, if they were old in the year 1573, they may have come from a time when accurate knowledge of Joanna's identity was still preserved by tradition. That John of Arundel had a daughter Joanna appears at least by his will, dated November 26, 1379, abstracted in *Testamenta Vetusta*. Nobody else could be the legatee called "my daughter Joan," the surname not being given, in the will of John of Arundel's widow, found among the Lambeth wills. The testatrix, originally a Maltravers, who brought that title to her said husband, calls herself "Alianor Arundell," although she had married, secondly, Sir Reginald Cobham. This instance of the retention of former name points to the possibility that when, in a will dated September 6, 1401, her daughter-in-law, Agnes de Arundel, speaks of "my sister lady Brian," Lady Brien may have indeed been already married to Echyngham: for Sir William Echyngham and a Joanna his wife had a charter in second year of Henry IV. (between September 30, 1400, and September 30, 1401). It scarcely was a former wife. Sir William had a wife whose name is given as Alice in Howard's *Miscell. Geneal. et Heraldica*, Vol. II., and who is said therein to have had daughters only; and one of these daughters we find in the will of his son Thomas Echyngham as "Domine Elizabeth Lewkenore sorori mee," while Thomas Hoo, apparently Elizabeth's son by her former husband, was made an executor. Sir William de Brien of Kemsyng married a daughter of John of Arundel, and died without issue, and Joan the widow had dower allotted to her December 12, in 21st year of Richard II. (1397). Now, did Sir William Echyngham marry this widow? and was she the Joanna buried with him and with her son Thomas in Echingham church? If so, the date of her death on the monument, viz., September 1, 1404, is probably wrong, being twenty-five days before September 26 in 5th year of Henry IV., which is the date of her mother's will leaving her some trinkets. An error of a month was not unlikely by the time the monument was erected, more than forty years after Joanna's death, doubtless pursuant to her son's will "corpus meum ad sepeliend. in Cancell. beate Marie Virginis de Echyngham juxta sepulturam domine Johanne matris mee." In those days the method of denoting the colors on coats-of-arms by lines, dots, etc., had not been invented, or at least was not in use, and on the aforesaid monument there is nothing to show the colors, which would have settled the question of her identity, if the reader thinks that any remains; but the monument, with the figures inlaid in brass, of Sir William, Joanna, and Sir Thomas, "filius eorum," has still decipherable an escutcheon impaling as her arms: quarterly, first and fourth, a lion rampant, and, second and third, fretty of six; which were the bearings of Fitz Alan and Maltravers respectively, and appear on the Garter plate of William, son of John of Arundel, "fretty" being a fret in the description in Burke's *General Armory*. The wife's half of the impaled shield on the monumental brass of Sir William de Brien, former husband of Joanna Arundel, has been described in a genealogical work as follows: quarterly, first and fourth, gules, a lion rampant or, and, second and third, sable, fretty or, the colors being perhaps denoted by letters. Boutelle's *Heraldry Historical and Popular* has a drawing of the seal of Joanna's nephew or great-nephew John, Earl of Arundel, where the fret, composed of six pieces, covers its quarters of the shield, and may be said to be fretty.

The lives of the Earls of Arundel, with carefully prepared tables of the family, are given in Tierney's *History and Antiquities of the Castle and Town of Arundel*. Thomas Echyngham, son of William and Joanna, is said, in the tabular view of Lord Windsor's ancestry, to have married Margaret, daughter of Sir Thomas Knivet, or Knyvett, and by her to have been father of the next Thomas: but this I am unable to verify. The volume on the Echynghams says that he married twice, one wife being the lady aforesaid. He certainly married Margaret, widow of Sir Thomas Marny, who died about 1414; a lease preserved in the Public Record Office, and appearing in the *Catalogue of Ancient Deeds*, printed by the Record Commission, dated February 20, in the 18th year of Henry VI., from John Marny, excepts the part of a manor assigned as dower to Margaret, wife of Thomas de Echyngham, Kt., late wife of Thomas, brother of said John. This Margaret, who was evidently then in the enjoyment of the dower estate, was probably mother of the second Thomas Echyngham, who, being over twenty years of age at his father's death, was born in 1423 or 1424, and, doubtless, the "wife Margaret" mentioned in the first Thomas Echyngham's will.

That the second Thomas Echyngham married Margaret, daughter of Reginald West, Lord de la Warr, which Margaret is said in Betham's *Tables* to have married Sir Thomas Erpingham, is stated in the tabular view aforesaid, and in some of the genealogies of the Echynghams before mentioned. On this point they are better authority than concerning Joanna, because more nearly contemporary; but the proof is also an escutcheon on the husband's monument. The wife of the second Thomas is represented by quarterly, first and fourth, gules, a lion rampant between six cross crosslets or, and, second and third, azure, three leopards' heads jessant fleurs-de-lis or, that being the description written in 1776. The more honorable quarters are given to the maternal line of La Warr, ancient rolls of arms showing the barons of that family to have borne gules crusily and a lion rampant argent, while the second and third quarters have the old arms of Cantelupe, which Sir Thomas West bore about the years 1392-97. The descent of Reginald West from Thomas of Brotherton, son of King Edward 1., by the daughter of the French king, is given in Betham's *Genealogical Tables of the Sovereigns of the World*. Various old accounts of the Mowbrays are silent as to the second John, Lord Mowbray, having any daughter who married De la Warr; and I was inclined to believe the latter's wife a daughter of the first John, although none such appears in any of the old accounts. De la Warr's daughter, who married West, could have been born, even if posthumous, no later than June, 1371, and De la Warr's wife at that time could not have been eighteen years old, if she was daughter of the second John, Lord Mowbray; for the latter's wife was thirteen years and perhaps a few months old in 1353. According to one account of the family, John himself was born in 1340; so, if that is correct, his being the father of De la Warr's wife is barely within the possibilities. I had intended omitting this descent from the chart, but have found in the *Lives of the Berkeleys*, by John Smyth of Nibley, prepared about 1630, and recently published, the mention of a manuscript at Berkeley Castle, written in the time, Smyth says, of William, Marquess Berkeley, who married another daughter of Reginald West, Elizabeth, sister of Margaret Echyngham, alleging that such marriage was nullifiable, because of near relationship, inasmuch as both William and Elizabeth were descended from the second John, Lord Mowbray, and Elizabeth Segrave, and giving the descent of Margaret's sister as I have given Margaret's in the chart. William, Marquess Berkeley, was great-grandson of the second John, Lord Mowbray, and Elizabeth Segrave, and inherited lands as a co-heir of the blood of Thomas of Brotherton, and was surely informed, and could have communicated to the person from whom the manuscript may have emanated, as to whether a particular person was descended from his own great-aunt. Were it not for this manuscript, or if it could be supposed to have been the incorrect statement of a stranger, the descent from St. Louis of France would be stricken out, but there would remain the possibility of De la Warr's wife being daughter of the first John, Lord Mowbray, and so descended from St. Louis's father. Were the entire descent of Margaret Echyngham who married Blount from Louis VIII., as well through Joanna, Sir William Echyngham's wife, as through De la Warr's wife aforesaid, to be stricken out, there could still be traced a legitimate descent of Edith, daughter of Lord Windsor, from Chilperic of Burgundy and his son-in-law Clovis; for Raymond Berenger, Count of Provence, father-in-law of Henry III. of England, was also descended from Sancho III., King of Navarre, called Emperor of Spain. This last descent is omitted for want of space. Margaret Echyngham may have been the child of an earlier wife of Lord De la Warr than Margaret Thorley, and so only half-sister of Elizabeth Berkeley: but there is no evidence that he had an earlier wife, and Dugdale's *Addenda*, quoting Vincent's Collections, make all the children to have been by Margaret, dau. of Robert Thorley, mentioning among them Margaret, and stating her to have married Thomas, Lord Echyngham. The son and heir was by Margaret Thorley, notwithstanding what some works on the peerage say; for Legh, in his *Accedens of Armorie*, mentions the Lord De la Warr of Henry VIII.'s time as bearing the arms of Thorley. In corroboration of what has been obtained from other sources, Hasted's *History and Topograph. Survey of the County of Kent*, says: Thomas Echyngham died without male issue, and Margaret, his only (this is incorrect, there being two daughters) daughter, carried the manor of Jacques Court in marriage to Sir William Blount, Kt., eldest son of Sir Walter Blount, Lord Mountjoy, who died before his father, leaving one son Edward and two daughters, and Edward, after succeeding to the estate, died without issue, and on a partition one of the sisters, Elizabeth, carried it to her husband Sir Andrew (*sic*) Windsor, whose son William sold it.

When we treat of the Plantagenets and their connections, it is hardly necessary to specify the standard authorities which have been followed, much less to go over the work of writers who have gathered full information from public archives and contemporary histories. Where the lines in this chart have been carried past England into Continental Europe, I have decided every step by the great authority of *L'Art de Vérifier les Dates;* and that part of this work, except the Byzantine genealogy derived from Du Cange, is wholly extracted from the same.

CHARLES P. KEITH.

321 South Fourth Street,
  Philadelphia, July 1, 1893.

THE ARMISTEAD FAMILY.

There is a tradition that the Armisteads derive their name and origin from Darmstadt; and the seat of the elder line in Virginia was called "Hesse." Without deciding when or whether in modern times they crossed the German Ocean, it is sufficient to say that they were Englishmen for several generations before William Armistead came to America, the name, with varied spelling, frequently appearing in Yorkshire records of the time of Queen Elizabeth. The emigrant to America seems, from the names of his children, Anthony and Frances, to have been the son of Anthony "Armitstead" of Kirk Deighton, Yorkshire, and Frances Thompson of the same place, who obtained a marriage license in the year 1608. On August 3, 1610, "William ye son of Anthony Armsteed of Kirk Deighton" was baptized in All Saints' Church, the only church in the parish. Search for a few years later discloses the fact that this child, whom I suppose the emigrant, passed safely through the period of tender infancy; at least no burial can be found. His father continued to reside there, having other children, and a contemporary named Thomas Armsteed, who also had a family. The emigrant's marriage did not take place there, if, as I assume, it was later than 1627, and prior to 1634. William "Armestead" received a patent in 1636 from Captain John West, Governor of Virginia, for 450 acres in Elizabeth City County, lying southeast upon the land of Mr. Southell, northeast upon the land of John Branez (Branch?), easterly upon the creek, westerly into the woods; among the persons he had transported to the colony being his wife Anne. The name is spelt "Armstead" in a patent of 1651. As far as I can learn, he had the following issue, probably by the same wife, and probably born in America:

 William Armistead, his heir-at-law, who patented land, and d. s. p., his brother John being his heir,

 John Armistead, the Councillor, and ancestor of both Presidents Harrison, see next page,

 Anthony Armistead, see p. 18,

 Frances Armistead, d. 1685, m., 1st, Rev. Justinian Aylmer, and, 2nd, Anthony Elliott, Lieut. Col., who d. about Jany., 1665-6, and, 3d, Christopher Wormeley, Colonel, step-son of Governor Sir Henry Chicheley.

It is difficult to give a complete account of the earlier generations of a Virginia family, owing to the transmission of real estate by the law of primogeniture, and the destruction or inaccessibility of records. For what follows, there is evidence derived from the best genealogical sources at my command.

JOHN ARMISTEAD, the Councillor, son of the emigrant, is called brother by Robert Beverley, but it is impossible to say whether one married the other's sister or the sister of the other's wife. Beverley was married twice. It is uncertain whether Armistead had any other wife than Judith, said to have been a Bowles in an article in *The Standard*, published in Richmond; but, this being probably a distortion by tradition of the marriage of his grandson into that family, her parentage is unknown.

Issue, as far as I can learn:

 JUDITH ARMISTEAD, m. Robert Carter, see below,
 ELIZABETH ARMISTEAD, m., 1st, Ralph Wormeley, and, 2nd, William Churchill, see p. 15,
 WILLIAM ARMISTEAD, m. Anna Lee, see p. 16,
 HENRY ARMISTEAD, m. Martha Burwell, see p. 17.

JUDITH ARMISTEAD, whose tombstone calls her "eldest daughter of the Hon. John Armistead, Esq., and Judith his wife. She departed this life the 23d day of February, Anno, 1699, in the —— year of her age, and in the eleventh year of her marriage, having borne to her husband five children, four daughters and a son, two whereof, Sarah and Judith Carter, died before and are buried near her," m. (1st w. of) Robert Carter,—the latter's daughter who married Benjamin Harrison, and was ancestress of the Presidents, was by the 2nd wife.

Issue:

 ELIZABETH CARTER, m., 1st, Nathaniel Burwell, and, 2nd, George Nicholas, M.D.,
  Issue by 1st husband, see Bedell and Burwell notes,
  Issue by 2nd husband, besides others:
   Robert Carter Nicholas, Treasurer of Va., m. Anne Cary, and was father of, among others, Wilson Cary Nicholas, Gov. of Va., and Elizabeth, who m. Edmund Randolph, U. S. Secretary of State,
 SARAH CARTER, d. y.,
 JUDITH CARTER, d. y.,
 JUDITH CARTER, m. (2nd w. of) Mann Page of "Rosewell,"
  Issue, besides three who died young:
   Mann Page, m., 1st, Alice Grymes, and, 2nd, Anne Tayloe,
   John Page, of "North End," m. Jane Byrd,
   Robert Page, of "Broadneck," m. Sarah Walker,
 JOHN CARTER, Secretary of the Colony, m. Elizabeth Hill of "Shirley,"

Issue:
    Elizabeth Carter, m. (1st w. of) William Byrd,
    Charles Carter, of "Shirley," m., 1st, Mary W. Carter, and,
      2nd, Ann B. Moore,
    Edward Carter, of "Blenheim," m. Sarah Champe.

ELIZABETH ARMISTEAD, dau. of the Councillor, d. Nov. 16, 1716, m., 1st, (acc. to Hayden's *Virginia Genealogies*, Feb. 16, 1687) Ralph Wormeley, Secretary of the Colony, whose will is dated Feb. 2, 1700, and, 2nd, Oct. 5, 1703, William Churchill. In the marriage contract dated Sep. 4, 1703, Robert Carter, Esq., William Tayloe of Richmond Co., William Armistead of Gloucester Co., and Christopher Robinson and John Robinson of Middlesex are called "uncles" of her Wormeley children.

  Issue by 1st husband:
    JOHN WORMELEY, said in Hayden's *Virginia Genealogies* to have been born in 1689, and d. 1726, and father of, among others, Ralph Wormeley, member of the Council, who was grandfather of Ralph Randolph Wormeley, Admiral in British Navy,
    JUDITH WORMELEY, d. Dec. 12, 1716, in 22nd y. of her age, m. about Aug., 1712, (1st w. of) Mann Page,
      Issue:
        Ralph Page, b. Dec. 2, 1713, d. unm.,
        Maria Page, called Judith Page after her mother's death, b. Feb. 24, 1714–5, m. William Randolph of "Tuckahoe," and had, among others (see Page's *Genealogy of the Page Family in Virginia*), Thomas Mann Randolph, who m. Anne Cary, from whom descend Wilson Miles Cary of Baltimore, great-grandson, Mrs. Burton N. Harrison, great-grand-daughter, Thomas Jefferson Coolidge, U. S. Minister to France, great-grandson, etc., etc.,
        Mann Page, b. Dec. 8, 1716, d. Dec., 1716,
  Issue by 2nd husband:
    ARMISTEAD CHURCHILL, b. at "Rosegill," Middlesex Co., July 25, 1704, d. in or after 1757, m. Hannah, dau. of Nathaniel Harrison (see notes on that family),
      Issue:
        William Churchill, b. Feb. 24, 1726, of "Bushy Park," and afterwards of "Wilton," Middlesex Co., ancestor of Mrs. Noland, now of Olfley, Va.,
        John Churchill, b. Dec. 1, 1728,
        Nathaniel Churchill, b. June 16, 1730, d. Dec. 21, 1730,
        Henry Churchill, b. Nov. 16, 1731,
        Armistead Churchill, b. Nov. 25, 1733, removed to Ken-

tucky in 1787, grandfather of Samuel B. Churchill, Sec. of State of Ky.,

Betty Churchill, named in Hayden's *Virginia Genealogies*,

Lucy Churchill, b. Jany. 17, 1737-8 or 1738-9, two entries of her birth and baptism in parish records,

Priscilla Churchill, named by Hayden,

Judith Churchill, b. Nov. 21, 1743,

PRISCILLA CHURCHILL, b. Dec. 1, 1705, d. in or after 1757, m. —— Lewis,

ELIZABETH CHURCHILL, named last in her father's and her mother's wills, baptism not mentioned in records of Christ Church, Middlesex Co., d. at "Eltham," April 16, 1779, in her 70th year, m., 1st, Jany. 29, 1729, William Bassett (see notes on that family), and, 2nd, (2nd w. of) Rev. William Dawson, D.D. (Oxon.), Pres. of William and Mary, and Commissary, who d. 1752,

Issue by 1st husband:

Elizabeth Bassett, b. Dec. 13, 1730, m. Benjamin Harrison the Signer, and was mother of, among others, Pres. William Henry Harrison,

others, see notes on Bassett family,

Issue by 2nd husband:

unknown, it appearing that Thomas Dawson and Rebecca Dawson, who m. Wilson Miles Cary, were not stepbrother and step-sister, but nephew and niece of Mrs. Harrison.

WILLIAM ARMISTEAD, son of John, p. 14, is supposed to have been older than Henry, because mentioned without him in the marriage contract between his sister and Churchill, resided in Gloucester Co., m. Anna, d. after 1753, dau. of Hancock Lee by his w. Mary, dau. of William Kendall (see Hening's *Statutes at Large*, Vol. VI.).

Issue:

JOHN ARMISTEAD, whose will, in 1734, names children, and speaks of them as minors, m., 1st, Elizabeth ——, called "sister" by James Burwell in his will, and, 2nd, Susanna, dau. of Thomas Merewether of Essex Co.,

Issue by 2nd wife:

John Armistead, of Gloucester Co., gent., living in 1754,

William Armistead, living in 1754,

Susanna Armistead, may have been by 1st wife, m. in or before 1753 Moore Fauntleroy,

JUDITH, not certain that she was an Armistead, but Burwell calls her "sister," m., before date of Burwell's will, George Dudly,

MARTHA, called "sister Martha Burwell" by James Burwell, may have m. Lewis Burwell,

MARY ARMISTEAD, m., 1st, James Burwell (see notes on that family), d. 1718, aged 29, and, 2nd, Philip Lightfoot,—it is not known that Burwell had any other wife than Miss Armistead, and his will mentions two children : Nathaniel Bacon Burwell and Lucy Burwell,—Lightfoot resided in York Co., and by will dated July 31, 1749, mentions three sons, John, Armistead, and William, the first of whom died without issue, and a law was passed in 1769 docking the entail of Armistead Lightfoot's lands, Hening's *Statutes*, Vol. VIII.,—

Issue by 2nd husband :
John Lightfoot (perhaps by another wife), d. s. p.,
Armistead Lightfoot, living 1769, m. Anne, living in 1769,
William Lightfoot (apparently the youngest, perhaps by another wife).

HENRY ARMISTEAD, son of John, p. 14, resided in Gloucester Co., and was mentioned in Col. Edmund Berkeley's will, dated Dec. 4, 1718, and d. after 1739 (?), appears to have married Martha, daughter of Lewis Burwell (see notes on the Bedell and Burwell families).

Issue :
WILLIAM ARMISTEAD,—newspaper of 1739 mentions marriage of Mr. William Armistead, son of Col. Henry Armistead of Gloucester Co., to a dau. of James Bowles dec'd, one of the Council of Maryland, and grand-dau. of Tobias Bowles, formerly a merchant in London in the Virginia trade. The will of James Bowles, styling himself "of St. Marys County in the Province of Maryland, merchant," dated June 13, 1727, probated January following, mentions daughters Eenor (*sic*) Bowles, Mary Bowles, and Jean Bowles, and wife Rebecca and uncle George Bowles. The Eleanor before mentioned, m., 1st, William, son of Gov. Sir Wm. Gooch of Va., and, 2nd, Warner Lewis, the tombstone of her son Warner Lewis, who d. Dec. 30, 1791, aged 44, calling him "eldest son of Warner Lewis and Eleanor Gooch, widow of William Gooch and the daughter of James Bowles of Maryland." James Bowles's wife Rebecca appears in note to *Official Records of Robert Dinwiddie* as having m., 1st, —— Bowles, brother of General Bowles of the British Army, and as being a daughter of Thomas Addison by his w. Elizabeth, dau. of Thomas Tasker, Treas. of Maryland. The will of William Armistead, dated Dec. 30, 1755, names the following sons (see Hening's *Statutes*),—

Issue :
William Armistead,

John Armistead, doubtless the one who m. (Mch. 17, 1764, Appendix to Meade) Lucy Baylor, and was ancestor of Lewis Armistead, Gen. C.S.A., who fell at Gettysburg,
Bowles Armistead,
Henry Armistead,
ANNE ARMISTEAD (called in *The Standard's* article on Walke family the daughter of Capt. William Armistead of Eastmost River, Gloucester Co., but I do not find any Anne in James Burwell's will, so conclude she was Henry's daughter), m. April 4, 1725, Anthony Walke,
LUCY ARMISTEAD (called in *The Standard* of Sep. 18, 1880, the dau. of John and Martha (Burwell) Armistead, no doubt Henry's dau.), m. Thomas Nelson, Sec. of the Council, for whose descendants see Page's *Genealogy of the Page Family in Virginia*,
ROBERT ARMISTEAD (called the son of John and Martha (Burwell) Armistead, may have been one of these children), m., 1st, after 1750, Elizabeth, wid. of Jeduthun Ball, and dau. of Charles Burgess, and, 2nd, Ann Smith,
Issue:
Henry Armistead of Fredericksburg, d. s. p., m. ―― Peachy, perhaps others, including those said in *The Standard* to have been children of John and Martha (Burwell) Armistead.

ANTHONY ARMISTEAD, son of the emigrant, resided in Elizabeth City Co., and was Major and Burgess, living in 1699, m. acc. to deed dated July 18, 1698, Hannah, dau. of Robert Ellyson of James City Co. She was named in her son William's will, and her own will was probated, Dec. 19, 1728. For information as to this branch, I am indebted to Pres. Lyon G. Tyler of William and Mary College.
Issue:
WILLIAM ARMISTEAD, m., 1st, Hannah Hinde, and, 2nd, Rebecca Moss, see p. 19,
ANTHONY ARMISTEAD, m. Elizabeth Westwood, see p. 20,
ROBERT ARMISTEAD, m., 1st, ―― Booth, and, 2nd, Katherine Sheldon, see p. 21,
JUDAH, or JUDITH, ARMISTEAD, m., 1st (license Oct. 15, 1695), John West of New Kent Co., who received land from his father-in-law Capt. Anthony Armistead, July 18, 1698, and, 2nd, ―― Butts,
Issue by 1st husband:
Charles West, owner of West Point, York River, will dated Sep. 28, 1734, calls Judith his mother, d. s. p.,
HANNAH ARMISTEAD, m. (license Dec. 10, 1698) William Sheldon,
DUNN ARMISTEAD, of whose estate an inventory was filed in 1716, may have been son of Anthony, and appears to have died d. s. p.

WILLIAM ARMISTEAD, page 18, resided in Elizabeth City Co., and was Major, Burgess, and Justice, will dated Jany. 5 (year blank), probated Feb. 17, 1715–6, m., 1st, before Nov. 20, 1696, Hannah, b. July 1, 1673, dau. of Thomas Hinde (or Hine) by his w. Hannah, Mrs. Hinde marrying subsequently John Powers and Pasco (or Pascho) Dunn. Major Armistead m., 2nd, Rebecca, dau. of Edward Moss, Moss's will probat. Dec. 17, 1716. She married about 1719–1720, John King, and her will is dated Feb. 13, 1755, probat. Aug. 1, 1758.

Issue by 1st wife:

JOHN ARMISTEAD, conveyed Nov. 29, 1769, land which descended to him by the death of his brother Hind, m. —— Gill, of New Kent Co.,

Issue:

Starckey Armistead,

William Armistead, Captain, m. ——,

Issue:

Gill Armistead, mentioned in 1791,

John Armistead,

Gill Armistead, m. Elizabeth Allen,

Issue:

Elizabeth Armistead, m. Miles Selden, Major, her cousin,

Susanna Armistead, m. (2nd w. of) John Cary of Elizabeth City Co.,

—— (dau.) Armistead, m. —— Russell,

WILLIAM ARMISTEAD, will probat. June 21, 1727, m. Judith ——.

Issue:

Dunn Armistead,

William Armistead, m. Constance ——, and appears to have been the William who m. Judith Bray Inglis, dau. of James Inglis by his w. Anne, dau. of Jean Marott, that William and Judith having son Henry, b. Jany. 8, 1753,

Issue:

Henry Armistead, b. Jany. 8, 1753,

Judith Armistead, mentioned in Judith Robinson's will as dau. of nephew William Armistead, may have been dau. of this Wm.,

Anne Armistead,

Frances Armistead,

Simon Armistead,

Henry Armistead,

ANTHONY ARMISTEAD, in 1737 sold lands descended from his mother, "daughter of Mr. Thomas Hine," will probat. 1741, m. Margaret ——,

Issue:

William Armistead, may have been father of Judith,

John Armistead,

Anthony Armistead,
Benil Armistead,
HIND ARMISTEAD, d. s. p., m. Hannah, wid. of Mathew Watts,
Issue by 2nd wife:
Moss ARMISTEAD, d. s. p.,
EDWARD ARMISTEAD, will probat. Apr. 25, 1771, m., 1st, Jane, probably the "daughter Jane Armistead" of Elizabeth Moss's will probat. Mch. 21, 1736, and, 2nd, Martha ———,
    Issue, order and mother uncertain:
        Robert Armistead, b. Feb. 1737-8,
        Moss Armistead, b. May, 1740,
        William Armistead, named in grandmother's and aunt's wills, may have been father of "Judith dau. of nephew William Armistead," named in Mrs. Robinson's will,
        Anne Armistead, named in aunt's will,
        Edward Armistead, b. Apr. 3, 1749,
        Samuel Armistead, named in father's and aunt's will,
        Rebecca Armistead, b. Feb. 22, 1761, named in aunt's will,
ROBERT ARMISTEAD, named in mother's will, may have been father of "nephew James Armistead," whose daughter Anne is named in Mrs. Robinson's will,
HANNAH ARMISTEAD, b. after date of her father's will, named in grandmother's, m. (1st w. of) Miles Cary of "Pear Tree Hall," Warwick Co., County Clerk,
    Issue appearing in Mrs. Robinson's will:
        John Cary, b. about 1745, of Elizabeth City, named in grandmother's and aunt's wills, d. 1795, m., 1st, Sally Schlater, and, 2nd, Susanna, dau. of Gill Armistead of New Kent,
        Robert Cary, named in said wills, d. in Buckingham about 1803,
        Rebecca Cary, m. Rev. Miles Selden, who d. 1785,
        Elizabeth Cary, m. Benjamin Watkins,
JUDITH ARMISTEAD, b. after her father's will, named in grandmother's, d. s. p., her will dated Mch. 16, 1768, probat. Jany. 27, 1769, m. before date of her mother's will John Robinson.

ANTHONY ARMISTEAD, son of Anthony, p. 18, was Colonel, Sheriff, Burgess, and Justice, will probat. Dec. 18, 1728, m. Elizabeth, sister of William Westwood.
Issue:
    WESTWOOD ARMISTEAD, m. Mary, dau. of John and Mary Tabb,
    ANTHONY ARMISTEAD, to whom his father left land purchased of Dunn Armistead, and left by Pascho Dunn, and who is said in *The Standard* to have removed to North Carolina,
    HANNAH ARMISTEAD.

Robert Armistead, son of Anthony, p. 18, was of York Co., Captain, Sheriff, and Justice, will probat. May 9, 1742, m., 1st, —— Booth (?), and, 2nd, Katharine, dau. of Thomas Nutting, and wid. of his brother-in-law William Sheldon.

  Issue by 1st wife:

    Ellyson Armistead, of York Co., Captain, Justice, etc., will probat. Dec. 19, 1757, m. Jane, dau. of Rev. Charles Anderson, Minister of Westover,

      Issue:

        Robert Booth Armistead, of York Co., m. Christiana, b. Dec. 23, 1745, dau. of James Shields, Colonel, by his 2nd w. Anne, dau. of Jean Marott,

          Issue:

            Mary Marott Armistead, m. John Tyler, Judge, and was mother of John Tyler, President of the United States,

        Ellyson Armistead,

        James Bray Armistead,

        Frances Anderson Armistead,

        Jane Armistead,

        Elizabeth Armistead,

    Booth Armistead, received a legacy from Thomas Booth, and d. 1727,

  Issue by 2nd wife:

  Robert Armistead,

  Booth Armistead, will probat. Jany. 24, 1771,

    Issue:

      Robert Armistead,

      Betty Armistead,

      John Armistead,

Angelica Armistead.

BACON.

WHEN, in 1676, Nathaniel Bacon raised the revolt against the Governor of Virginia, and made himself memorable in the name "Bacon's Rebellion," by which the revolt has been known, an older Nathaniel Bacon, a near relative, was a member of the Governor's Council. The "rebel" was expected to be the heir of this childless namesake, but died before him; and the namesake in 1688 became President of the Council, and, as such, the chief magistrate of the colony. Dying on March 16, 1691-2, he left the bulk of his property to the Burwells. I do not know what proof there is that his wife was a Kingsmill, as Bishop Meade says. That name may have been given to the Burwell seat for a different reason. The Burwells of "Kingsmill" were not descended from Bacon's niece. William Bassett (see notes on that family) called Nathaniel Bacon "brother." Bassett was not a step-brother, and did not marry a Bacon, but a Cary (see Bassett and Cary notes); so I conclude that Bacon married a Bassett, probably dead before August 28, 1671, when Bassett made his will. Bacon's wife whose death occurred November 2, 1691, in her 67th year, Elizabeth, was the widow of Colonel William Tayloe of King's Creek, York County, as is recited in a deed from the latter's heir-at-law to Lewis Burwell, who at her death procured a warrant of escheat for land devised to her by said husband (communicated to me by Wilson Miles Cary, Esq., of Baltimore).

The arms on the tomb of Nathaniel Bacon are those borne by some of his forefathers, viz.: quarterly, Bacon and Quaplad.

The tombstone of Lewis Burwell the second of that name in Virginia, calls his first wife "Abigail Smith of the family of the Bacons;" and her tombstone, which does not give her own name of Smith, says, "who was descended of the illustrious family of the Bacons, and heiress of the Hon. Nathaniel Bacon, Esq., President of Virginia." Nathaniel's tomb says that his "descent was from the Ancient House of ye Bacons (one of whom was Chancellor Bacon and Lord Verulam)." According to the rest of the inscription, he had been in Virginia over forty years; so that he could not have arrived later than 1651. The will of Rev. James Bacon, Rector of Burgate, Suffolk, England, is among the *Bury Wills and Inventories* published by the Camden Society, and when compared with the will of this Nathaniel Bacon, identifies him with the clergyman's son of that name; and the inscription on the tombstone of Rev. James Bacon tells us that the latter was son of Sir James Bacon, Kt., prior to whom we can get information as to the genealogy from Kimber and Johnson's *Baronetage of*

England, supported by the *Visitation of London*, Stow's *Survey of London*, etc. The ancestry has been carried much further than will be found in the Chart, but prior to John, the father of Robert, there is a contradiction between the different accounts as to Christian name. As far as the Chart gives it, the relationship of the Bacons prior to Sir James appears in wills of which I have obtained abstracts. As to the father-in-law of Sir James, *i. e.*, Francis Bacon, and Francis Bacon's parentage, wife, and only daughter, we are informed by a brass effigy of him in Pettistree Church. The wills of Francis's father and grandfather have been examined, and make that part of the Chart certain.

The records of Friston Church give the baptism of "Nathaniel Bacon, eldest son of Sir James Bacon, Knight," and his birth, May 15, 1593, and his burial, August 7, 1644. The baptism of Nathaniel's daughter Elizabeth, October 9, 1628, is mentioned, but not that of his son Thomas, who was father of the "rebel." The "rebel," being great-nephew of Rev. James, was first cousin once removed of Nathaniel Bacon, President of the Virginia Council, and second cousin of Abigail Smith, who married Lewis Burwell.

The statement in the *New England Hist. and Geneal. Register*, Vol. XXXVII., that Rev. James Bacon's daughter Martha, who was unmarried on September 24, 1647, the date of her father's will, married a Mr. Smith of Colchester, led to finding in the register of St. James's Church, Colchester, the entry of Abigail Smith's baptism, with date of birth, calling her the daughter of Anthony Smith and Martha, his wife. The will of the father confirms the identification. Anthony Smyth of Colchester, tanner, speaks of his two eldest daughters, Anna and Martha, and makes the eldest, Anna, evidently by a former wife, executrix, with the care of the three youngest children, Elizabeth, Abigail, and George; and speaks of the lands which were to be divided between Mrs. Burroughs, Mrs. Wilkinson, and said George after "Mrs. Peckes her death my Mother in Lawe;" and appoints Mr. Thomas Burroughs of Bury St. Edmunds, as one of the supervisors. The latter was the son-in-law named in Rev. James Bacon's will, Mrs. Burroughs and Mrs. Wilkinson were two of Rev. James Bacon's daughters, and the son George was the heir of the third daughter, then deceased, while the widow of Rev. James Bacon had become Mrs. Peck. Mr. Henry F. Bacon of Aldershot, England, sends me a copy of a memorandum to the effect that Rev. James Bacon by his wife "Martha Honeywood," had a daughter Martha, who married ———— Smith of Colchester, and by him had a son and heir, George Smith, aged 14 in 1666. It will be seen further on that Honeywood or Honywood was not the maiden name of Mrs. Bacon. Anthony Smyth (or Smith)'s daughter, called "Elizabeth Sherry sister of aforesaid Abigail" in Nathaniel Bacon's will, doubtless married her cousin, son of the man whom Smith calls "my brother, Mr. Thomas Sheriff of Diss in Norfolk," who, Blomefield tells us, was greatly respected and beloved, a Justice of the Peace in the days of the Commonwealth, who had saved many Royalists from ruin. The following inscription, recorded by Blomefield, may be that of Mrs. Burwell's sister: "M. S. Elizabethæ Johannis Sheriffe, hujus Oppidi dudum Incolæ nec non Medici inclyti Viduæ pientissimæ, Quorum Sobolis Pietas Parentnm Moribus imbutæ hoc Monumentum poni voluit. Illa autem, pacificâ spe Beatæ Resurrectionis ad Vitam sempiternam, Naturæ Debitum solvit Anno Actatis 46, Nov. V, 1702." The arms impaled on the tomb with those of Sheriff are described as a chevron between three roundels, and Burke's *General Armory* gives many instances of Smiths bearing a chevron between three roundels (bezants or plates), with crosses pattée fitchée on either chevron or roundel, or some such variation. It is to be regretted that we can not positively say which wife of Rev. James Bacon was Mrs. Smith's mother, although the mention of Martha after Elizabeth in his will makes it probable that Martha was younger than Elizabeth, and we know that the latter was a child of the wife who survived him. That wife, moreover, was, like Mrs. Smith, named Martha. She was not a Honywood, but a daughter of George Woodward of Buckinghamshire, by his second wife, Elizabeth Honywood. Both the Woodwards and Honywoods were well known families. The mother of George was a Boulstrode, and the mother of Elizabeth was the celebrated Mrs. Honywood, whose maiden name was Atwater or Waters. Stories are told of the latter's religious melancholy, and she was memorable for the great number of her progeny, having 16 children, 114 grandchildren, and 228 great-grandchildren up to her death in her 93d year, May 16, 1620, her only husband, Robert Honywood, having died April 22, 1576. One of her grandsons was Sir Robert Honywood of Cromwell's Council of State, and another was Sir Thomas Honywood of Cromwell's Other House, which took the place of a House of Lords, while a son of Sir Robert was Sir Philip Honywood, a Royalist, who came to Virginia in 1649, but afterwards returned to England, selling his land in Virginia to William Bassett, who called Nathaniel Bacon his "brother," and made him an executor of his will. In Harl. MS. 1533, f. 4, is a pedigree of the Woodwards, originally prepared in the latter part of the XVIth Century, but continued in a later handwriting about 1637. It traces the family to John Woodward, whose son George was clerk of the castle of Windsor. George's son John had by his wife Margaret, daughter of George Boulstrode "of higher Bowlstrod in Com. Buck," a son, George Woodward, who m., 1st, "Kath: daur. of Tho. Wodford of Brightwell," and, 2nd, "Elizab: da. of Honewod of Marks Hall in Essex." The pedigree gives the following issue of George Woodward by the first of these wives:

"Edward Wodward of Upton now Liveing, 1634" = "Elizab: sister of Sr. Robt. Oxenbridg of Husborne in Hampshire ob. 20 March, 1637,"
 Issue:
  "Edward Wodward Eldest = Katherine, daur. of Tho. Marsh de Warsley in Com. Huntingdon

John 2
Wm 3
Georg slayne at the seig of Mastrike in ye Low contries
Lucy 1
Elizab: 2
Anne 3"
"Thomas Wodward of Lincolns Inne dyed sans issue
"John ma: ye da: of Manfield,"
Which John was living at the date of his stepmother's will, and his wife's name was Bridgett.

The marriage license of George Woodward, "gent.," and Elizabeth Honywood, "spinster, of the City of London," was granted December 9, 1579. The pedigree aforesaid gives them the following issue:
"Margaret mar. to Sr. Jon. Ashburnham srvant to ye Q. of Bohemia
Bridgett mar. to Sr Tho Lydall & after to Tho: Heneage
Sara mar. to Agar of Staffordshire
Henry dyed young
Robert dyed young
Isaack dyed young
Mary mar. to Thomas Eccleston of Winchelsey
Elizabeth mar. to Thomas St. Nicholas of Kent
Anne Ma: to Doctor Sheff Prebend of Windsor
Rebecka Mar. to Weston
Rachell Mar. to Giles Poulton of Lond. Mrchant
Martha Mar. to Mr. Bacon of ———."

The will of Elizabeth Woodward, mother of the above named, is dated August 3, 1631, and mentions her daughters St. Nicholas, Lydall, Poulton, Ashburnham, Sheaffe, Bacon, and Agard, her son-in-law Sir John Ashburnham, her "son" Dr. Sheaffe, and her "son Poulton;" and leaves to a number of persons, among them her grandsons, Thomas Lidall and Edward Sheaffe, and two god-daughters, "Elizabeth, daughter of my said daughter Rachel Poulton," and "Elizabeth, daughter of my said daughter Martha Bacon." This last bequest shows us that Elizabeth, first named among Rev. James Bacon's daughters in his will before mentioned, was the child of the wife who survived him, who is called in some church notes, prepared about 1655–1665, in the British Museum, "dau. of Honeywood Esq. She was grandchild of that famous Mrs. Honeywood so often made mention by devises (sic) in regard to her long distress of conscience and brought up by her. The husband of Mrs. Honeywood was a man of £3000 per annum in those times. She was, after the death of Mr. Bacon, married to Mr. Robert Pecke, Rector of Hingham in Norff., a woman of singular parts." So we have the marriage of Rev. James Bacon and Martha Woodward at least as early as 1629; for not only was Elizabeth born, but the records of Burgate show the baptism on November 18, 1631, of "Anna, filia Jacobi et Marthæ Bacon." This Anne was the last named daughter in her father's will. The Honywood MSS., published in the *Topographer and Genealogist*, make it clear that Martha Woodward, whose marriage is not mentioned by the original compiler, had no children at the death of her grandmother Honywood, and, as there are entries therein of the year 1622, unlikely that Martha was married before 1623; so Nathaniel Bacon, President of the Council of Virginia, was not her son, for he was born about 1619. If the Rev. James was intended by Lady Anne Drury, when, in her will dated June 1, 1621, published among the *Bury Wills and Inventories*, she left 20l. to "my cosen James Bacon and his wyfe to bestowe in some plate to remember me,"—Lady Anne Drury and Rev. James being children of first cousins,—it can be supposed that the latter's first wife was still living. One of the witnesses to the will was "Martha Bacon:" the first wife may have had the same Christian name as the one who survived him. I do not know the date of birth of Mrs. Smith; her baptism does not appear in the register of Burgate or of the other parishes where it seemed likely to have taken place. While the probability is that she was daughter of Martha Woodward, it is not proved by Anthony Smyth's use of the term "mother-in-law," which could have meant stepmother-in-law.

Sir Thomas Lyddal, Knt., called "Sr Tho Lydall" above, name now Liddell, was the eldest son of Thomas, and is said in Collins's *Peerage of England* to have died in 1627, "in his father's lifetime, leaving issue by Bridget (who was maid of honour to the Queen of Bohemia), daughter of Edward (sic) Woodward of Lee, near Windsor, Esq., one son Sir Thomas." Collins adds, "(She was secondly married to Thomas Heneage of Battersea in Surry, Esq., nephew of Sir Thomas Heneage, Knt.)" Thomas Lyddal, the father of Bridget's first husband, had a fifth son, George: was not this the resident of York County, Virginia, who was co-executor of Bassett's will with Nathaniel Bacon, Esq.? Sir Robert Peake, Kt., citizen and goldsmith of London, in his will dated May 15, 1666, abstracted in *New England Hist. and Geneal. Register*, Vol. XXXVII., leaves 300l. to "my cousin and sometime servant George Lyddall, in Virginia, gentleman." Another Bacon family or branch of this Bacon family came to Virginia; and Lyddall appears among the Christian names subseqnently borne by them.

BASSETT.

Mrs. Lewis Washington (Ella Bassett) has kindly given me the benefit of certain family papers in her possession, including a copy of the will of the second William Bassett in the Chart, the first of the family who came to Virginia. Styling himself "of the Parish of Blissland, County New Kent, gentleman," he desires to be buried in the upper church of that parish " by my dear wife and boy," by which, I am confident, he meant wife and son then living. The rest of the will is to the following effect: " my nephew Joseph Foster" land purchased of John Pouncey, being a neck between Diascou and Mr. Richmond Terrill's, New Kent, "a Virginia forty foot house" to be built for him upon this, and " the middle silver tankard" and a couple of silver spoons; "unto his two sisters Anne and Mary Foster" 6000 lbs. each of tobacco when of age or married; "to my mother Mrs. Anne Dickeson;" " to my sister Mary Scott . . . all my interest in a house in New—— [rest of word does not appear] in the Isle of Wight in which my mother now lives near the town gate;" "wife Bridgett Bassett, the house and land I now live on formerly bought of Charles Edmonds" for her life, and " the housing due to me as intermarrying with her or by me purchased of Emanuel Wills who married her sister Elizabeth," or if said house should be sold by an order formerly given to Mr. Simon Hurle, the proceeds to be paid to said Bridget; to only son William Bassett, tract bought of Col. Robert Abrahall and John Brock, being 1800 a., and 1200 a. adjoining taken up by testator; and, if son die, to nephew Joseph Foster, residuary estate to son, and, if he die under eighteen, two-thirds to wife, and one-third to Joseph Foster, and, if he die under age without issue, to his said sisters or the survivor. The executors were " my deare Brother Nathaniel Bacon, Esqr." and George Lyddall. The will was dated Aug. 28, 1671, witnessed by said Abrahall and Brock, and proved by their oath on Jany. 4, 1671-2. A very great amount of time and trouble has been expended by me in endeavoring to ascertain the testator's ancestry. The name of his descendants' seat, "Eltham," suggested that he sprang from James Basset, gentleman of the Royal Chamber, who died in 1558, and his scholarly wife Mary, daughter of William Roper of Eltham, in Kent, England. Mary's mother was a daughter of Sir Thomas More, Lord Chancellor of England, who, moreover, had descendants in Virginia, spelling their name Moore, and calling their seat " Chelsea," after the suburb of London, which was his residence. Strange to say, the will of William Roper mentions no Bassets; and any will of James Basset's widow, I have been unable to find. James Basset's will mentions a son Philip, and provides for an expected child. An unsigned pedigree appearing in the Supplement to the *Visitation of Devon, 1620*, published by the Harleian Society, says that James had a son Philip, who had daughters, leaving us to infer that the name in that branch became extinct: but this is not conclusive; nevertheless, I can not find the grandchildren of James. Burke's *Landed Gentry* says that James had two sons, Philip and Charles, and, as the former was a " Popish recusant," I am inclined to think that Charles was the Dr. Carolus Bassettus, or Bassett (the genitive case is given), whose two servants were among the Englishmen in Rome in 1582, as appears in a list published in *Collectanea Topographica et Genealogica*. The pedigree aforesaid omits the four younger sons of Sir Arthur Basset of Umberley by his wife Elinor Chichester. Of these four sons, Arthur was knighted in Ireland by his uncle, the first Lord Chichester, when Lord Deputy, and d. s. p. 1640, I having a copy of his will; another, Francis, obtained in 1624 by the influence of his uncle, the second Lord Chichester, a captaincy under Count Mansfeldt; another, William, was matriculated at Oxford in 1603, aged twenty, but did not take his degree; and John, the youngest, born in 1585, survived Arthur, and was administrator d. b. n. of the latter, being probably also a resident of Ireland, but I can not trace him further. John, it would seem, married; for his uncle, the first Lord Chichester, in his will dated Mch. 8, 1624, leaves to not only Sir Arthur Bassett and Francis Bassett, but also " the little wenche Peggye Basset."

It is rather odd that the names Abrahall and Foster, which occur in the emigrant Bassett's will, appear with Bassett of Beaupre and Basset of Ewley, among the persons marrying into the Denis family, flourishing about this period, descended from the Berkeleys, in Smyth's *Lives of the Berkeleys;* and that Col. Henry Norwood, hereafter mentioned as a friend of the emigrant, belonged through a female line to the Denises. Basset of Ewley, I have traced down, and perhaps as to Bassett of Beaupre, whose name is spelt with two t's, like the emigrant's, there is only a coincidence. The arms on the tomb of the emigrant's son and on silver of the family, are barry wavy, or three bars wavy, and a chief: three bars wavy being the arms given in the Supplement to the *Visitation* aforesaid for the Bassets of Umberley, and barry wavy being now borne by their representative. The inscription on the aforesaid tomb calls the emigrant " William Bassett Esqr. of ye County of Southampton in ye Kingdom of England," perhaps to distinguish him from another William Bassett in Virginia, step-son of William Felgate. Newport being the chief town of the Isle of Wight, and the emigrant's mother, Anne Dickeson, being at the date of the emigrant's will a resident of a town there of which the first part of the name was New, there is no doubt that the emigrant was son of William Bassett " of Newport, yeoman," on whose estate letters of administration were granted Feb. 28, 1647, to Anne the widow, as appears at Winchester,

England. From the silence of the parish register at Newport, which has no entry of the family prior to the baptism of Richard, son of William, Aug. 15, 1642, I suppose that William and Anne removed thither from some other part of the shire, a number of Bassetts appearing in the records of Winchester. Neither will nor any administration on the estate of Mrs. Dickeson has been found. As the emigrant married a Cary, which is proved by the wife of Wills being her sister (see notes on the Cary family), it is evident that besides Mary Scott and the mother of the Fosters, probably distinct from Mary Scott, there was a sister of the emigrant who had married "Brother Nathaniel Bacon," and in addition to these there was an "Anne Dafter of Will Bassate" baptized at Newport, May 27, 1646, and buried in 1648, in the entry of which burial the father's name is correctly spelt. The father's burial appears on Dec. 4, 1646.

James Waylen's recent work *The House of Cromwell and the Story of Dunkirk* has some amusing instances how, after the Restoration, participants in the previous struggle on the Republican side were credited by family tradition with more fashionable principles, and transmitted to remoter posterity as Royalists. It might have instanced Sir Bryce Cochran, who is said in Douglas's standard *Peerage of Scotland* to have been killed in the king's cause in 1650, but who appears in Waylen's work as an officer in 1658 in the very successful expedition sent by Cromwell against Dunkirk. In the list, Aug. 17, 1659, of captains to be commissioned in Sir Bryce's regiment, called Sir Brian's, published among the *State Papers*, appears William Bassett. There was also a lieutenant named William Bassett, but the emigrant is frequently spoken of as Captain in the Virginia records. Col. Henry Norwood and Sir Philip Honywood (as to which latter, see notes on the Bacons) had been among the Royalists who came to Virginia in 1649. Both returned to the Old World. Norwood was made Deputy-Governor of Dunkirk in March, 1661-2, and saw Bassett there. The place was, by treaty between Charles II. and Louis XIV., delivered to France; and was evacuated Nov. 18, 1662. Norwood was afterwards at Tangiers. In a letter, William Bassett, the emigrant, thanks Norwood for advice to him on leaving Dunkirk. Bassett saw Sir Philip Honywood at White Hall, and there agreed with him, or reached a final agreement, to purchase land belonging to Honywood in Virginia, as appears by papers in possession of Mrs. Washington.

The issue of the second William Bassett in Virginia of this family were:
MARTHA BASSETT, b. Dec. 28, 1694,
ELIZABETH BASSETT, b. July 4, 1697,
LUCY BASSETT, b. May 24, 1699,
JOANNA BASSETT, b. Oct. 12, 1701, d. Oct. 25, 1702,
JOANNA BASSETT, b. Oct. 2, 1703, d. Oct. 4, 1708,
WILLIAM BASSETT, b. Mch. 27, 1705, d. Sept. 8, 1708,
LEWIS BASSETT, b. Aug. 10, 1707, d. Sept., 1708,

WILLIAM BASSETT, b. July 8, 1709, m. Elizabeth Churchill,
BURWELL BASSETT, b. Mch. 3, 1712,
HANNAH BASSETT, b. Mch. 9, 1713-4, m. Peter Hack,
MARY BASSETT, b. Aug. 7, 1716, d. (tombstone) Aug. 23, 1753 or 1755, m. Edward Huck Moseley, Colonel, and was ancestress of S. Bassett French, of Manchester, Va., Judge, etc.,
NATHANIEL BASSETT, b. Jany. 16, 1718-9.

The issue of William Bassett, Burgess in 1743, and d. 1744 (?), by his wife Elizabeth Churchill, were:
 ELIZABETH BASSETT, b. Dec. 13, 1730, m. Benjamin Harrison the Signer,
 WILLIAM BASSETT, in memorial of whom there is a little locket in the Harrison family, inscribed " Wm. Bassett obt 17th Feb. 1737 Æt. 5,"
 BURWELL BASSETT, m., 1st, Anne Chamberlayne, and, 2nd, Anna Maria Dandridge, see below,
 PRISCILLA (?) BASSETT, m. —— Dawson,
 Issue:
  REBECCA DAWSON, d. s. p., m. (2nd w. of) Wilson Miles Cary, who d. 1817,
  THOMAS BASSETT DAWSON, a midshipman in Virginia State Navy during Revolutionary War, wounded while bearing despatches, bounty land awarded to the Bassetts, Stiths, Harrisons, etc., as heirs of uncles and aunts of his sister, who was his heiress, d. s. p. after the Revolutionary War,
 JOANNA BASSETT, d. before 1818, m. John Stith,
 Issue:
  BASSETT STITH, of Halifax Co., N. C., Colonel, d. 1817, m. Mary ——,
  Issue:
   Lavinia Stith, d. before 1835, m. Robert Newsum,
   Issue:
    Mary B. Newsum,
   Martha E. Stith, d. before 1835, m. John R. J. Daniel,
   Issue:
    William Augustus Daniel, b. after 1813,
    John Daniel,
    Julius Daniel,
   Maria B. Stith, m. Joseph J. Daniel,
   Mary M. Stith, m. Edmund B. Freeman,
   Virginia P. Stith, m. Nathaniel M. Eaton,

William Anderson Stith, b. after Jany. 1, 1795,
Albert Augustus Bassett Stith,
Nicholas L. B. Stith,
Sarah Frances Stith,

JUDITH BASSETT, d. s. p. before Rebecca Cary, m. Peter Lyons, Judge of Va. Court of Appeals,

perhaps others, d. s. p., it being said that there were a Frances and a Nancy, both d. unm.

BURWELL BASSETT, of "Eltham," frequently a member of the House of Burgesses, was active as a patriot during the Revolution, d. Jany. 4, 1793, m., 1st, when he was 19, Anne, dau. of John Chamberlayne. If she had issue, the same died young. He m., 2nd, May 7, 1757, Anna Maria, b. Mch. 30, 1739, d. Dec. 17, 1777, dau. of John Dandridge, and sister of Martha Washington.

Issue, all by 2nd wife:

ELIZABETH BASSETT, b. Jany. 21, 1758, d. s. p., her or the second Anna Maria's death in Mch., 1773, spoken of in letter of George Washington,

ANNA MARIA BASSETT, b. May 16, 1760, d. July 23, 1760,

WILLIAM BASSETT, b. Sep. 19, 1761, d. 1775,

ANNA MARIA BASSETT, b. Feb. 26, 1763, d. s. p.,

BURWELL BASSETT, b. Mch. 18, 1764, of "Eltham," member of Congress for many years, d. s. p. 1841, m., 1st, ———, dau. of Daniel McCarty, and, 2nd, Ann Claiborne,

JOHN BASSETT, b. Aug. 30, 1765, m. Betty Carter Browne, see p. 32,

GEORGE BASSETT, b. Aug. 7, 1766, d. same day,

FRANCES BASSETT, b. Dec. 19, 1767, d. within a year after 2nd marriage, m., 1st, 1785, George Augustine Washington, d. 1793, nephew of George Washington, President of the United States, and, 2nd, (2nd w. of) Tobias Lear, George Washington's secretary,

Issue by 1st husband (none by 2nd):

Child, d. y. before George Washington's letter to Sir Isaac Heard,

ANNA MARIA WASHINGTON, d. before 1840, m. ——— Thornton,

Issue:

Churchill Thornton, of Wilkinson Co., Miss., in 1839,
Charles Thornton, of Wilkinson Co., Miss., in 1839,

GEORGE FAYETTE WASHINGTON,

CHARLES AUGUSTINE WASHINGTON, d. s. p., George Washington's will speaking of Charles Augustine and Lawrence Augustine, so there may have been one of the latter name born after May 2, 1792, date of letter to Heard, but d. s. p.

JOHN BASSETT, b. Aug. 30, 1765, before mentioned, grad. William and Mary, lawyer, resided at "Farmington," Hanover Co., Va., d. 1826, m., Sep. 12, 1786, Betty Carter Browne, dau. of William Burnet Browne, of Salem, Mass., afterwards of "Elsing Green," King William Co., Va., descendant of Rt. Rev. Gilbert Burnet, Bp. of Salisbury. William Burnet Browne's wife was Judith Walker Carter, dau. of Charles Carter, of "Cleve."
 Issue:
  VIRGINIA BASSETT, b. Sep. 20, 1787, d. before her father, m. Sep. 20, 1806, Samuel W. Sayre,
   Issue:
    Philip Ludwell Sayre, d. y.,
    Edward Sayre, d. unm.,
    Burwell Bassett Sayre, dec'd, m., 1st., —— Theobald, and, 2nd, Mildred Ruffin,
     Issue:
      Virginia Sayre,
      Elizabeth Sayre,
    Stephen Sayre, b. Dec. 10, 1812,
    William Sayre, b. Feb. 22, 1814, dec'd, m. —— Gadsden, of So. Car.,
     Issue:
      A son,
    John Bassett Sayre, b. Mch. 24, 1817, d. y.,
  ANNA MARIA DANDRIDGE BASSETT, b. Mch. 15, 1789, d. before May 15, 1839, m., 1st, Joseph Deans, and, 2nd, Isaac Garretson,
   Issue by 1st husband:
    J. S. Deans,
   Issue by 2nd husband:
    Daughter, m. —— Van Bibber (?),
  WILLIAM BASSETT, b. Oct. 10, 1790, d. Nov. 21, 1812,
  FRANCES CARTER BASSETT, b. Dec. 9, 1792, d. Jany. 4, 1795,
  JOHN BURWELL BASSETT, b. Dec. 27, 1794, d. Apr. 12, 1796,
  JOHN CHURCHILL BASSETT, b. May 1, 1797, d. Sep. 12, 1798,
  JUDITH CARTER BASSETT, b. Jany. 5, 1799, d. Aug. 21, 1800,
  GEORGE WASHINGTON BASSETT, b. Aug. 23, 1800, m. Betty B. Lewis, see below,
  BURWELL BASSETT, b. Jany. 22, 1802, d. Oct. 1, 1802,
  HENRY ALFRED BASSETT, b. Nov. 17, 1803, d. aged 15 mos.,
  ALFRED BASSETT, b. July 18, 1805, d. Sep. 25, 1805,
  BETTY CARTER BASSETT, b. Jany. 5, 1807, d. s. p., m. Samuel Buckus, of "Malvern Hill."

GEORGE WASHINGTON BASSETT, b. Aug. 23, 1800, of "Eltham,"

"Farmington," and "Clover Lea," d. Aug. 28, 1878, m. his cousin Betty Burnet Lewis, dau. of Robert Lewis by his w. Judith Carter Browne, sister of George Washington Bassett's mother. Robert Lewis was son of Fielding Lewis, and nephew of George Washington.

Issue:

    Betty Bassett, m. Ronald Mills,
    Georganna Bassett, d. inf.,
    George Washington Bassett, d. unm. Aug., 1886,
    Virginia Bassett, dec'd, m. John H. Claiborne, and left four children,
    Ella Bassett, m. Lewis Washington, and has had a son and a daughter, the latter dec'd,
    Frances Carter Bassett, m. C. T. Mitchell, and has six children,
    Mary Bassett, m. Benjamin Harrison Bassett, son of William Bassett of Louisiana, and left eight children,
    Annette Bassett, dec'd, m. Rev. J. E. Ingle, and had two sons,
    Robert Lewis Bassett, m. Sallie Jeffries of Benham, Texas, and has one son,
    William Augustine Bassett, d. unm.

BEDELL AND BURWELL.

By a deed dated July 28, 1648, found by W. G. Stanard among the records of York County, Va., Dorothy Wingate, relict of Roger Wingate, Treasurer of Virginia, conveyed to "her well-beloved son Lewis Burwell" all rents due at said Roger's decease, and confirmed to her by the King. The *Visitation of Bedfordshire with Additional Pedigrees* (the latter prepared in 1637), published by the Harleian Society, tells us that Roger Wingate, living in London in January, 1637, married Dorathey, dau. of William Bedell of Catworth, County Huntingdon, widow of Edward Burwell of Harlington, County Bedford. The records of Great Catworth covering a long period were examined for me by the Rector; and, while the marriage of William Bedell was not found, having probably occurred in Northamptonshire, the baptism of his daughter Dorothy was. Some entries of the surname in the records aforesaid are followed by the word "generosus," indicating the rank of the family; and the inquisition upon the death of the William Bedell who is called "of Moldesworth" in Camden's *Visitation of Huntingdonshire*, printed by the Camden Society, identifies him as at one time styled "of Catworth Magna." So the paternal line of Dorothy, the mother of the first Lewis Burwell, can be traced to a John Bedell of Wollaston, Northamptonshire, who died in 1485, with whom the pedigree in Camden's *Visitation* starts. The inquisition mentions several sons of William Bedell, besides Silvester, his heir, who alone is mentioned in the *Visitation*, and, among them, Henry Bedell, who is called "brother" in Edward Burwell's will; and the name of the last wife of William was Elizabeth, the *Visitation* calling his wife Bridget Power of Northamptonshire.

Blaydes's *Genealogia Bedfordiensis* has extracts from parish records relating to the Burwells, from which we find that Edward had the following children, the word "gent." appearing in each entry after the father's name:

EDWARD, bapt. at Houghton Conquest, Apr. 14, 1616, bu. at Ampthill, Mch. 4, 1620,

DOROTHY, bapt. Ampthill, June 24, 1618, perhaps m. —— Woodington, as Elizabeth Vaulx conveyed land to her "kinsmen" John and Charles Woodington about 1657,

ELIZABETH, bapt. Ampthill, February 25, 1620, probably m. Robert Vaulx or Vause, of London and some time of Virginia, merchant, who made a power of attorney to his "brother" Lewis Burwell, and whose wife about 1656 is called Elizabeth,

LEWIS, bapt. at Ampthill, Mch. 5, 1621, the first of the name in
    Virginia,
GEORGE, bapt. at Ampthill, May 17, 1624,
EDWARD, bapt. at Ampthill, Feb. 19, 1625.

The will of Edward Burwell was nuncupative, as follows:
"Oct. 18, 1626, Directions taken from my brother Burwell being upon his sick bed," desired that his children be brought up in the fear of God, left his whole estate to his wife Dorothy, desired his sister Sheafe to take his eldest daughter, and keep her as servant, and his sister Wingate to take his daughter Elizabeth, entreats Lord Bruce to consider his faithful service to him, his brother Wingate to be overseer, and with him his brother Henry Beadles (sic) and Mr. Edward Blofield : Witnesses, John Orpin Clerke (clerk?) and Edward Wingate. Letters of administration were issued to Dorothy, the widow, on Nov. 9, 1626. Probably this Edward Burwell was the one baptized at Toddington, Aug. 24, 1579, described as son of Edward ; and, while possibly the son of another wife, was no doubt the son of the Edward Burwell, called "Edmund" in one copy, who is mentioned in the *Visitation of Bedfordshire* aforesaid as having married Jane, daughter of Edmond Wingate of Sharpenhoe, by his wife Mary, dau. of Wm. Belfield (*Qu.* the same name as " Blofield" in the will?). The "sister Wingate" in the will was Jane Burwell, married at Maulden, Aug. 25, 1619, to Edward Wingate; she is called in the *Visitation* the daughter of Edw'd Burwell of Harlington, County Bedford, and that her mother was a Wingate appears from George Button's will, dated Dec. 4, 1618, before Jane's marriage, mentioning his "brother Wingate's niece Jane Burwell." " Edward Burwell, gent.," apparently this Jane's father, and Lewis's grandfather, was buried at Ampthill, Nov. 19, 1620. Can we doubt that he was the one who is named in the Charter dated May 30, 1609, commonly called " the Second Charter," to the Virginia Company?

The tombstone over the first Lewis Burwell says " descended from the ancient family of the Burwells of the counties of Bedford and Northampton in England, who nothing more worthy in his birth than virtuous in his life," etc. The family of his father-in-law, Higginson, I have not succeeded in tracing, although it is described as "ancient." Burwell's widow Lucy, by her third husband, Philip Ludwell, who had been Governor of Carolina, had (see *New England Hist. and Geneal. Register*, Vol. XXXIII.) a daughter, who m. Daniel Parke of Virginia, killed while Governor of the Leeward Islands, and a son Philip, of the Virginia Council, who m. Hannah Harrison. Allowing for step-relations helps us to explain Governor Spotswood's complaint that the Council embraced too many of one family. He says in one of his published *Letters* that six out of the ten members were related to Ludwell, who, as has been shown above, was step-uncle of the Burwells; and, on Mch. 9, 1713, probably having in mind some persons like Nathaniel Harrison, whose brother had married a Burwell, declares: "The greater part of the present Council are related to the Family of the Burwells. . . . If Mr. Bassett and Mr. Berkeley should take their places, there will be no less than seven so near related that they will go off the Bench whenever a Cause of the Burwells come to be tryed."

The second Lewis Burwell by Abigail Smith (see notes on the Bacon family), his first wife, had according to her tombstone four sons and six daughters. They were probably as follows, the parents' marriage not likely to have taken place before 1671, Nathaniel Bacon, in his will dated Mch. 15, 1691-2, naming those then living:

JANE BURWELL, probably died before Mrs. Bassett's birth, bu. near her brothers Lewis and Bacon (see Bp. Meade's account of tombs at Carter's Creek), not named in Nathaniel Bacon's will,

JOANNA BURWELL, b. 1675 (?), called "eldest daughter" on her husband's tomb, meaning probably eldest surviving, d. Oct. 7, 1727, in her 53rd year, m. Nov. 28, 1693, William Bassett (see notes on that family),

ELIZABETH BURWELL, d. Monday (month blank) 30, 1734, over 50 (last part of the year of her age illegible,—I suggest in 57th year), m. Benjamin Harrison (see notes on that family),

BACON BURWELL, not named as one of the children then living in Nathaniel Bacon's will, buried at Carter's Creek,

NATHANIEL BURWELL, b. 1680 or 1681, called "eldest son" on his tomb, probably meaning eldest surviving, will dated Aug. 20, 1721, d. 1721, in his 41st year, m. Elizabeth, dau. of Robert Carter, she afterwards m. George Nicholas, M.D. (see notes on the Armistead family),

Issue:

Lewis Burwell, Pres. of the Council of Virginia, d. before Mch., 1772, m. Mary, dau. of Francis Willis,

Issue:

Lewis Burwell, eldest son by said wife, living 1772 (see Hening's *Statutes*),

Rebecca Burwell, m. Jaqueline Ambler, their dau. m. Chief Justice Marshall,

.others,

Carter Burwell, of "The Grove," m. Lucy Grymes,

Issue:

Nathaniel Burwell, of "Carter Hall," Clarke Co., Va., who m., 1st, Susanna Grymes, and, 2nd, Lucy, widow of Geo. W. Baylor, dau. of Mann Page of "Rosewell,"

perhaps others,

Robert Burwell, of Isle of Wight Co., d. in or after 1769, m. about 1742, acc. to Page's *Genealogy of the Page Family in Virginia*, 2nd edition, Sally, step-sister of Pres. Nelson of the Virginia Council, and of Secretary Nelson of the Council,

    Issue:

        Nathaniel Burwell, of Lancaster Co., m. Miss Wormeley,

        Frances Burwell, m. (1st. w. of) Gov. John Page,

Elizabeth Burwell, m. William Nelson, Pres. of the Council of Virginia, and was mother of, among others, Thomas Nelson, Signer of the Declaration of Independence,

LEWIS BURWELL, b. 1682 (?), d. Sep. 16, 1696 (probably the correct year, but Bp. Meade says 1676), in his 15th year, which is more likely than 5th year, for he is mentioned in Nathaniel Bacon's will between Nathaniel and James, as among the children then living, and there could have been but one Lewis by the first wife, to make the number of four sons,

One daughter, died before Mch. 15, 1691-2, the date of Nathaniel Bacon's will,

LUCY BURWELL, d. (Meade) Dec. 16, 1716, in 33rd year, m. Dec. 1, 1704, Edmund Berkeley, member of the Council,

MARTHA BURWELL, probably the young lady with whom Gov. Nicholson fell madly in love, swearing that if she married any one else, he would cut the throat of the bridegroom, the minister, and the justice who gave the license, the result of the matter being his removal from office, m. Henry Armistead (see notes on that family),

JAMES BURWELL, b. 1690 (?), whose tombstone says that he d. Oct. 6, 1718, in his 29th year, his own will dated Sep. 6, 1718, m. Mary Armistead (see notes on that family), but she may have been a 2nd wife,

    Issue:

        Nathaniel Bacon Burwell, d. in or before Nov., 1769,

            Issue:

                James Burwell (see Hening's *Statutes*),

            perhaps others,

        Lucy Burwell.

By his 2nd wife, Martha, dau. of John Lear, a Councillor, and widow of William Cole, Burwell had two sons and eight daughters, of whom a son and two daughters survived him. Apparently both of these two daughters, whose names I do not know, had died before James Burwell made his will, unless one of them was Judith, wife of George Dudly, she being called "sister" by Burwell, but she may have been sister of his wife.

The son could have been no other than the Lewis Burwell named in James Burwell's will. He was the one who resided at "Kingsmill" or "King's Mill," and d. in or after 1736, and is said to have married an Armistead, probably the "sister Martha Burwell" of James Burwell's will, and to have had two sons, viz.:

LEWIS BURWELL, of "Kingsmill," d. 1784 (4 Munford's *Rep.*), m. Frances, dau. of Edwin Thacker, entail of her lands being docked (Hening's *Statutes*, Vol. VI.), and was father of, among others, Thacker Burwell, who m. Mary Armistead, and had William Armistead Burwell (private secretary to Thomas Jefferson, President of the United States) and Edwin Thacker Burwell, who d. s. p.,—William Armistead Burwell, d. 1821, was grandfather of Miss Lettie M. Burwell of Bedford City, Va.,

ARMISTEAD BURWELL, see *The Standard*, published in Richmond, of June 18, 1881.

CARY.

THE inscription on the tombstone of Col. Miles Cary, the first of the name in Virginia, gives the name of his father, mother, and maternal grandfather. It calls him the "only son," which, I think, is incorrect, even if meaning the only son who attained full age. The ancestry of John Cary has been derived from a pedigree registered in 1699 in the Heralds' College, London, by John Cary of Bristol, England, gentleman, and his brother Richard Cary, Alderman of London, grandsons of an elder brother of said John. With the pedigree are filed copies of wills, etc., proving it. A confirmation of arms was duly granted in 1699, setting forth that the branch of the family seated at Bristol had "time out of mind" borne the arms of the family of Cary of Devonshire, viz.: argent, on a bend sable, three roses argent, with a silver swan for their crest (which arms are on the tombstone of Col. Miles Cary, the emigrant), and also that Robert Cary, Lord Hunsdon, had personally acknowledged them as kinsmen, and Edward Cary of Torre Abbey, Esquire, heir male and principal representative of the Devonshire family, had declared that he had heard that the Bristol Carys had sprung from a younger branch of the same.

Henry Hobson was buried in the Church of All Saints, Bristol, on March 29, 1635, and a funeral certificate was duly filed in the College of Arms. His coat-of-arms was: argent, on a chevron azure between three pellets as many cinque-foils argent, with a chief chequy or and azure. His will mentions Henry, Matthew, Richard, Miles, Alice, Mary, and Honor Cary, as children of John Cary of Bristol, draper, by the testator's daughter Alice.

"Father-in-law Thomas Taylor deceased" is mentioned in the will of the emigrant Cary, dated June 9, 1667, probated June 21, as well as "my loving wife," whose Christian name is not given. From deeds and patents, Wilson Miles Cary, Esq., of Baltimore, who has furnished me with nearly all the information I possess as to the family, finds that her name was Anne. The will directs two houses in Baldwin and St. Nicholas Streets in Bristol to be sold for the benefit of three daughters, Anne, Bridgett, and Elizabeth, when married. This property is doubtless "the housing" to which William Bassett (see notes on Bassett) in his will refers as having been acquired by marriage and purchase from Emanuel Wills; while Mr. Simon Hurle, mentioned by Bassett as having an order to sell the same, was doubtless the "Mr. Hurle" under whose guardianship Cary's son

Miles was at school in England, according to Cary's will. The son William was left to the care of Mr. William Beaty to be educated and brought up in Virginia. The overseers were "friends Mr. Thomas Ludwell, Coll. Nathaniel Bacon, Major Edward Griffith and Mr. Wm. Beaty." The emigrant died June 10, 1667, of wounds received in the attack by the Dutch fleet upon Old Point Comfort, where he had been ordered to build a fort in 1665. His tombstone at "Cary's Quarter," at the intersection of the James and the Warwick Rivers, enumerates his children: Thomas, Anne, Henry, Bridgett, Elizabeth, Miles, and William. Henry was ancestor of the Carys of "Ampthill," and Henry's great-granddaughter Anne m. Thomas Maun Randolph of "Tuckahoe" (see p. 15); Bridgett, daughter of the emigrant, m. about 1670 William Bassett; Elizabeth, her sister, m. Emannel Wills; and Miles was Burgess, Colonel, Surveyor-General, and Rector of the College of William and Mary, and was ancestor in the male line of Wilson Miles Cary, Esq.

HARRISON.

A TRADITION, mentioned by President William Henry Harrison, made him a descendant of the regicide General Thomas Harrison. It has not been generally accepted throughout the family, and is certainly untrue as far as it involves direct descent; for the regicide was a contemporary of the Harrison who emigrated to this country, and was probably a few years younger. If the tradition may be construed to mean that both were of the same family, we cannot at once reject it, finding it extant among the children of persons born within seventy years of the regicide's execution. That took place in October, 1660: Benjamin Harrison the Signer was born about 1726, and his brother Carter Henry Harrison a few years later; to one of the Signer's children the tradition has been traced as aforesaid, while Rev. Joseph Cabell Harrison, a descendant of Carter H., communicated the same to my correspondent, James Findlay Harrison of Kansas. Like other names ending in "son," which is supposed to indicate Danish origin, the name Harrison is very common in England: it was such as would be adopted by or applied to the children of numerous Harrys or Henrys not known to be related to each other. Until the present century, the regicide was the most celebrated person who bore it. Sprung from the yeomanry, he rose by his bravery and religious zeal until he held at one time, during Cromwell's absence, the command of the military forces in England. Best remembered as having the custody of the doomed King, but more important in the later days of the Commonwealth as the head or the hope of the "Fifth Monarchy" men, he met his own death with the fortitude and confidence of a martyr. After the Restoration, there would have been shame to acknowledge a relationship to him: after our Revolutionary War, there was temptation to imagine it. I have been unable to prove any between him and the Presidents' ancestor who came to Virginia; but I do not know the parentage of either. Although the historian Clarendon says that the regicide was born at Nantwich, Cheshire, which is about fifteen miles from Newcastle-under-Lyme, the latter, in Staffordshire, is generally supposed his birthplace. His father and himself certainly resided in Staffordshire. On April 11, 1648, he petitioned for the release of John Lawton of Lawton, Cheshire, which is nearer to Newcastle aforesaid than to Nantwich, speaking of him as his "loving neighbour." On Feb. 3, 1654, Harrison was ordered to retire to his father's house in Staffordshire, and Roger Williams, the founder of Rhode Island, in a letter of July, 1654, says that Harrison was confined within five miles of the elder Harrison's house, that is, not allowed to travel outside that limit, but had disobeyed the order. So the regicide's father was living at the beginning of the year, and there are other indications that, instead of being born in 1606, as has been stated (see *Dictionary of National Biography*, edited by Leslie Stephen), Harrison was still a young man at the breaking out of the Civil War, and under fifty when he suffered death. He resided in Staffordshire when the King's officers arrested him. Some Harrisons of that county, like others of the name elsewhere, claim descent from him. I have had a search made through the Harrison wills prior to the Civil War at Lichfield, where was an archidiaconal court having jurisdiction over Staffordshire, and no Benjamin is mentioned in any of them. If, as seems likely, the Virginia Harrisons came from another part of England, they may have been related to the regicide through his wife, who, as is shown in *Notes and Queries*, 6th Series, Vol. II., p. 383, was Catherine, daughter of Ralph Harrison, Esq., of Highgate, Middlesex. Of Ralph's early history I am ignorant: he was a colonel in the army, and left his widow the goodly annuity of £200.

Another interesting character of the name, and, moreover, one who, as far as age is concerned, may have been the father of the emigrant to Virginia, was John Harrison, soldier, religious writer, and agent to Sallee for the release of the English captives of the Emperor of Morocco, and who in 1622 was sent to the Somers Islands, or Bermudas, as Sheriff of that colony, and by the death of the Governor succeeded him, and was Governor during the early part of 1623. He is the one who has been called Governor of Virginia, from somebody's hasty glance at Capt. John Smith's *Generall Historie*, which treats of both Virginia and the Somers Islands. Those colonies in the XVIIth Century were closely connected, being at one time under the same Company; so that the genealogists who have started the line of Virginia Harrisons with that Governor are not proved wrong by his residence being in the Somers Islands instead of on the Continent, to which they were a half-way station. One is tempted to conclude that he was the ancestor or a near relation of the ancestor from the residence in those Islands, almost at the same time with him, of a Benjamin Harrison, who was probably the one who afterwards came to Virginia, and from John Harrison's son or nephew—he appears in the *State Papers* as nephew of John Harrison's sister—being named Peter Harrison, like the younger son of the emigrant to Virginia. I can find no tradition, however, to corroborate such a conclusion. Of John's parentage I am ignorant. He frequently spoke of himself as a poor "gentleman." His sister was in some way mother-in-law of Sir Jerome Lindsay, Lion King-at-Arms, whose first wife was a Colville, her parentage being unknown, and his second wife a daughter of Sir David Lindsay, Lion King. Sir Jerome was a son of David Lindsay, Bishop of Ross, who may have married Harrison's sister as his second wife. Sir Jerome had a son, Rev. David Lindsay, Minister of a church in Virginia, whose tombstone gives his father's name. Alexander Brown, in his *Genesis of the United States*, has made the mistake, not unnatural, of identifying the Governor of the Somers Islands with Sir John Harrison. The published *State Papers* tell us that the former had been a soldier in Ireland three years during Queen Elizabeth's reign, and a servant of Henry, Prince of Wales, for ten years, and that his wife was Elizabeth, daughter of Ambrose Wheeler, quarter-man in the King's service.

A number of Harrisons settled in Virginia in the XVIIth Century. The connection between but few of them is known. Those who emigrated before Benjamin the Clerk, apparently died without issue. Brown is right in making George, who was killed in a duel, the brother of Sir John. Very soon after 1640 appeared Thomas and Edward, the former figuring in Neill's works on Virginia history, first as Governor Berkeley's chaplain, and then as a non-conformist divine. They are mentioned also in Savage's *Genealogical Dictionary of New England*, as they resided there for some time. They are embraced in the following tradition, brought over from England by Rev. Joseph Harrison, a native of Skipton, Yorkshire, who lived in the city of New York in the early part of the present century, viz., four brothers of the name went to America, whom the Rev. Joseph Harrison called Thomas, Richard, Benjamin, and Nathaniel, of whom, his own father had told him, two went north and two south, a fifth brother, Edward, a clergyman, remaining in England, Cromwell being a member of his Church. Now, as we have seen, the name of the clergyman was Thomas, and he was one of those who came to America. Yet afterwards he preached in London, and accompanied Henry Cromwell to Ireland. Edward, too, was one of those who came to America. I can find no Nathaniel here at that time, nor any Benjamin in such registers in Yorkshire as have been examined; but the Richard of the tradition appears to be identical with the Richard living in New Haven in 1644: he may have been the father of Thomas, who was of New Haven in 1654, and of Branford in 1666 (one of whose sons was called Nathaniel), as well as of Richard, who had a son Benjamin, born in 1655. Four sons of Richard the younger, viz., John, Joseph, George, and Daniel, removed to New Jersey. Thus we have two brothers going to Virginia and two other branches of the family, descended from a third brother, settling in Connecticut and New Jersey. The Harrisons of the latter State claimed that one of their family went to Virginia, and a removal thither at the beginning of the XVIIIth Century is not improbable. Among the other Harrisons who came to Virginia were Dr. Jeremy and his wife Frances, the latter as a widow receiving in 1654 a patent for 1000 acres in Westmoreland Co. In 1655, 1000 acres were granted to her brother-in-law John Harrison in tail, remainder to her, remainder to Giles Brent of Peace in said county. The records of S. Runwald's Parish, Colchester, give us the baptism Dec. 31,

1610, of John, son of Sydney Harrison, and Dec. 31, 1612, of Jeremy, son of Sydney Harryson.

Benjamin as a baptismal name had some popularity in the century following the Reformation, or, rather, the revival of interest in the Old Testament. It does not argue relationship to find a number of Harrisons in the time of King James I. bearing the name of the youngest of the patriarchs. There was a Benjamin among the Harrisons of Northampton appearing in the *Visitation of Northamptonshire of 1619*, but there is no evidence that he was the emigrant to Virginia. He was of the generation born prior to the year 1600, so that he would not have been under fifty when the emigrant's eldest son was born. It would be gratuitous to assume that Benjamin, mentioned in the *Visitation*, had a son of the same name who was the emigrant to Virginia. The coat of arms was never claimed by the Virginia family. However, there is little argument to be made from coats of arms, when they first appear in the family several generations after the emigrant, as seems to have been the case with the Virginia Harrisons, who moreover at different times have used different ones. There is none on the tomb of the emigrant's son, and the arms on the tomb of the grandson, Benjamin of "Berkeley", are those of the Burwell family. On the tombstone of Mrs. Mary (Digges) Harrison, who died in 1744, and was the wife of the emigrant's great-grandson, is impaled gules, two bars sable between six estoiles placed three, two, and one; which with the difference of azure instead of gules are those of the Harrisons who for some time past have been seated at Copford Hall, near Colchester, Essex. It is noteworthy that there was a Benjamin among the brothers of John Harrison of St. Michael's, Wood street, London, who, by his will dated Feb. 19, 1638, devised lands "lately given unto me and my heirs by my grandmother situate in Læncc in the parish of Coppeford in Co. Essex," to his brother Francis and his heirs, and, in default of issue, to his said brother Benjamin in fee. This Benjamin lived at Aldham and Ipswich, Suffolk, and had a son of the same name, mentioned in the will of Judith Harrison in 1638, and of Robert Harrison in 1641; but I do not suppose the son old enough to have been Clerk of the Virginia Council about 1630; and perhaps both Benjamins are accounted for in the grant of letters of administration on the estate of persons of the name, one of Ipswich on Oct. 18, 1665, to his relict Susan, and the other "lately in parts beyond the seas, bachelor," on Sep. 26, 1682, to Thomas Younger, a creditor. The only Benjamin mentioned in the Harrison wills of Essex was the son of George by his wife Emma, Emma having died in or before 1616, as she was then spoken of as deceased by her mother Susan, who also had married a Harrison. This Benjamin survived the emigrant four years, being appointed in 1653 supervisor of the will of a brother George, and may have been the Benjamin Harrison of St. Sepulchre's, London, on whose estate letters of administration were granted on April 29, 1663, to his relict Elizabeth.

Perhaps it is better that a family so associated with the history of this country—even in its early existence as a group of colonies, each generation holding a respectable position in the government of the largest—should look to no other country as the field of any of its greatness, in fact, that its standing in the Old World should not be precisely known. It is not certain that even the name of the emigrant's father would have been ascertained if all the Harrison wills of the XVIIth Century in the British Isles could have been examined. There were, except in the days of the Commonwealth, a great number of probate courts, acting under the respective archbishops, bishops, archdeacons, etc., even in some localities under borough authorities. I have had such wills examined as my supposed clues called for, including all those of the name during certain periods in the Prerogative courts of Canterbury, and in those courts usually acting for London, Middlesex, Essex, Kent, Suffolk, Lincolnshire, Staffordshire, and Yorkshire, and can assert nothing. To have been employed as Clerk of the Virginia Council indicates that Harrison the emigrant had education and ability, and the sooner this happened after his arrival, the more likely that he had some early acquaintance with important persons in the colony or belonging to the Company. A clerk was appointed by the Governor or Council on the death or absence of the Secretary of the Colony. On June 11, 1621, the Virginia Company removed John Pory from the Secretaryship, and elected Christopher Davison, a brother of Francis Davison the poet, and a son of a Secretary of State under Queen Elizabeth (see Neill's *Virginia Carolorum*). Davison died, and in 1624 Edward Sharpless was made Clerk. He had not served much more than a year when he was removed, and his ears cut off, for disclosing public documents. On Mch. 4, 1625-6, William Clayborne was commissioned Secretary by the King. Clayborne was not in the Province when, about January, 1629-30, Governor Harvey arrived, bearing a commission dated Mch. 22, 1627-8, which also reappointed Clayborne as Secretary. Before Harvey's departure from England, a number of planters from the Somers Islands (now Bermudas) united in a petition presented to parliament on June 4, 1628, setting forth that most of them had lived there since the infancy of the plantation, *i.e.* for over six years, had lately brought to England their small means in tobacco, which had lain in the custom-house four months under a higher duty than it would yield, and they were in great necessity, some having been arrested for their board, and praying to have their tobacco by bills of store for the present year. There was a Ben Harrison joining in this petition; but, as all the names appended are in one handwriting, his signature can not be compared with that of the Clerk of the Virginia Council of that name. On the tobacco being released at a smaller duty, this Somers Islander may have transported himself to Virginia, a colony closely connected with the other. Nobody else appearing in the records as Clerk, he may have been employed as such as soon as William Clayborne left the colony, or he may have arrived with Harvey, and, the Secretary not being there, have been made clerk at the new Governor's suggestion. The influence of Capt. John Harrison, the agent to Sallee, would be an explanation, if indeed he was a relative. Harvey was a military character, and bore, like John Harrison, the title of "Captain," receiving knighthood on being appointed Governor. They probably met before Harvey sailed, which was subsequent to August 13, 1629; for Harrison made a petition on September 20. The time of Benjamin Harrison's appointment is calculated from the statement that he served several years. On Mch. 15, 1633–4, he certified to the copy of Abraham Piersey's will, signing himself "Ben Harryson, Clec. Con." In December, 1634, Richard Kemp, duly commissioned Secretary, arrived. There are no wills on record in the Bermudas prior to 1660. There is none of any Benjamin Harrison afterwards.

The earliest acquisition of land in Virginia by the emigrant was by deed from John Davis of Kiskiake, dated July 9 in ninth year of King Charles I., for 200 acres on Warrosquioake Creek, which, in a patent for it dated July 7, 1635, was said to be in the tenure of Thomas Jordan. Other patents followed, but "Berkeley" and "Brandon," the celebrated seats of the family on the James River, were acquired by later generations: "Brandon," as far as I can tell, by the emigrant's son; "Berkeley," by the first Harrison styled "of Berkeley" in the Chart, who may have inherited it through his maternal line. The operation of a mill probably made the emigrant's son a richer man than if he had been a mere planter. Benjamin of "Berkeley" was rich independently of his father, in whose lifetime he died, possessed of large tracts of land.

The first Harrison appears to have left but two children surviving him, Benjamin and Peter, both by his wife Mary, who afterwards married Benjamin Sidway; and as in a patent, dated Oct. 9, 1649, it is recited that 500 acres granted to Benjamin Harrison dec'd on Mch. 21, 1643, were due to Benjamin, Jr., as "his son and heir," we conclude, the law of primogeniture being in force, that Benjamin was the eldest son, and that the property belonging to Peter in his minority was not inherited, but devised to him, probably by his father, whose will has not been found. On Jany. 16, 1652, Benjamin Sidway, by order of Court, conveyed certain land belonging to "Peeter Harrison, orphan of Benjamin Harrison." In a patent dated 1655, quoted by *The Critic*, published in Richmond, certain land is said to adjoin that of "Peter Harrison, son of Benjamin Harrison deceased and son-in-law of Captain Sidney," the last word being doubtless "Sidway."

Peter Harrison appears to have died without issue before middle age, as he is not mentioned in the will of his mother, Mary Sidway, dated Mch. 1, 1687–8. It gives as follows: "Item. I give & bequeath unto my Grand Daughter Hannah Harrison the horse colt that sucks on the black mare. Item. I give & bequeath unto Jno. Kersey one yearling hepher. And for the rest of my estate my will is after my just debts paid that it be equally divided between my two sons Benja: Harrison and Tho: Sidway whom I do make my exors. to see this my will performed." The will was witnessed by Lyddeia Norwood and Sam'l Alsebrook, who proved it on May 29, 1688.

Thomas Sidway, half-brother of Harrison, appears to have died childless. His will, dated Jany. 16, 1694, probated Dec. 3, 1695, gives all his land and personal property to his wife Jeane for life, and at her death to William Stringer and his heirs. The wife was named as executrix, and the witnesses were Benj. Harrison and Sarah Pedington. Harrison also left something to William Stringer, if he came to this country, meaning probably that he had gone to England. So it is evident that he was nearly related to or connected with Sidway's and Harrison's mother. He appears to have been the William Stringer, of Charles City County, who Jany. 1, 1682, made Elias Osborne his attorney in the lawsuits between him and Wm. Pickerill and Thomas Hayard of Surry County. The witnesses to the letter-of-attorney were Paul Williams, John Harrisson, and George Jennings.

The tombstone of Benjamin Harrison of Surry, the Councillor, and Hannah his wife, gives the date of her birth and death, but not her parentage, and the destruction of so many of the public records and the incompleteness of family records prevent our discovering this. The late William Byrd Harrison of "Upper Brandon" was of opinion that she was a Churchill, but there is nothing to confirm this, and it may have been derived from the marriage of her granddaughter Hannah with Mr. Churchill.

The children of Benjamin Harrison the Councillor were:

SARAH HARRISON, of whose birth the date on the tombstone at Jamestown has been printed both 1670 and 1678, the latter being clearly wrong, as Hannah was born in that year,—If 1670 be correct, it shows that all the children, except perhaps Mrs. Edwards, but probably including her, were by wife Hannah, as Sarah is declared to have been, the tombstone saying: "She was daughter of Col. Benjamin and Mrs. Hannah Harrison of Surry. Born Aug. ye 14th, 1670 . . . died May ye 5, 1713, exceeding beloved and lamented." Sarah m. Rev. James Blair, D.D., Minister of Jamestown Parish, Commissary of the Bp. of London for Virginia, and President of the College of William and Mary, who survived her thirty years,—

BENJAMIN HARRISON, ancestor of the Presidents, b. about 1673, as we learn from his tombstone at Westover : " Hic Situs est in Spem Resurrectionis Benjamin Harrison de Berkeley, Benjamin Harrison de Surry Filius Natu Maximus, uxorem Duxit Elizabetham Ludovici Burwell Gloucestriensis Filiam & qua Filium Reliquit unicum Benjamin et unicam Filiam Elizabetham, Obijt Apr. x Anno Dom. MDCCX. Ætam XXXVII. . . .",

NATHANIEL HARRISON, whose tombstone, according to the Philadelphia *Evening Telegraph* of Mch. 13, 1890, was found on the north side of the James River Road near Sunken Meadow, Surry County, Va., with the following inscription : " Here lieth the body of the Hon. Nathaniel Harrison, Esq., son of the Hon. Benjamin Harrison, Esq. He was born in this parish the 8th day of August, 1677, departed this life the 30th day of November, 1727," appointed to the Governor's Council to succeed his father, resided at Wakefield, will dated Dec. 15, 1726, m. Mary Young, née Cary, supposed to have been Mary, born in 1678, daughter of John Cary, merchant of London, by his wife Jane, dau. of John Flood, of Surry County, Va.,

Issue :

NATHANIEL HARRISON, of " Brandon," m., 1st, Aug. 23, 1739, Mary, d. 1744, dau. of Cole Digges, and, 2nd, Lucy, widow of —— Fitzhugh,

Issue by 1st wife :

Benjamin Harrison of " Brandon," father of William Byrd Harrison of " Upper Brandon," see *Provincial Councillors of Pennsylvania, 1733–1776*, the account of the descendants of Edward Shippen therein to be republished by Miss Elise Willing Balch,

Elizabeth Harrison, m. John Thornton,

BENJAMIN HARRISON, of Wakefield, d. 1758, m. Aug. 23, 1739, Susanna, dau. of Cole Digges,

HANNAH HARRISON, m. Armistead Churchill, see notes on the Armistead family,

ELIZABETH HARRISON, m. before 1733 John Cargill of Surry County,

SARAH HARRISON, m. before 1733 James Bradby of Surry County,

ANNE HARRISON, m. Aug 9, 1739, Edward Digges, brother of her brother Nathaniel's 1st wife and of her brother Benjamin's wife,

MARY HARRISON, m. James Gordon, see Hayden's *Virginia Genealogies*,

HANNAH HARRISON, of whom there is this record, " daughter of Benjamin Harrison of Southarke Parish in Surry County in Virginia, Esquire, and Hannah, his wife, who was borne at Indian Fields in the said Parish the 15th day of December, 1678, and died April 4, Anno Dom. 1731," which daughter m. Nov. 11, 1697, Philip Ludwell, b. at Carter's Creek, Feb. 4, 1672, member of Virginia Council (see Bedell and Burwell notes), d. Jany. 11, 1726-7, son of Philip Ludwell, Governor of Carolina, and afterwards member of Virginia Council, by his wife Lucy née Higginson (see *New England Hist. and Geneal. Reg.*, Vol. XXXIII.),

Issue:

LUCY LUDWELL, b. Nov. 2, 1698, d. Nov. 2, 1748, m. John Grymes, Councillor,

HANNAH LUDWELL, b. Dec. 5, 1701, d. Jany. 25, 1749–50, m. Thomas Lee, Pres. of the Council of Virginia, commissioned Governor, but died before the commission arrived, Nov. 14, 1750,

Issue:

Richard Lee, b. June 17, 1723, d. unm.,

Philip Ludwell Lee, b. Feb. 24, 1726–7, one of whose daughters was 1st wife of Harry Lee, "Light-horse Harry," Gen. in the Revolution,

Hannah Lee, b. Feb. 6, 1727–8, m. Gawin Corbin, and had one daughter Martha, who m. George Richard Turberville,

John Lee, b. Mch. 28, 1729 (?), d. unm.,

Lucy Lee, b. Sep. 26, 1730, d. unm.,

Thomas Ludwell Lee, b. Dec. 31, 1731 (?), see genealogy in *New England Hist. and Geneal. Reg.*, Vol. XXVI., which is here followed with some correction of dates,

Richard Henry Lee, b. Jany. 20, 1732–3, proposed the resolution of independence in the Continental Congress,

Francis Lightfoot Lee, b. Oct. 14, 1734, a signer of the Declaration of Independence,

Alice Lee, b. June 4, 1736, m. William Shippen, M.D., of Phila.,

William Lee, Sheriff of London, agent of the Continental Congress at Nantes, m. Mch. 7, 1769, Hannah Philippa, dau. of his uncle Philip,

Arthur Ludwell Lee, b. Dec. 20, 1740, commissioner from the Continental Congress to France, Spain, and Prussia, d. unm., Dec. 12, 1792,

SARAH LUDWELL, b. July 29, 1704, d. Jany. 6, 1704–5,

PHILIP LUDWELL, b. Jany. 16, 1705–6, d. Mch. 9, 1705–6,

PHILIP LUDWELL, b. Dec. 28, 1716, d. Mch. 25, 1767, m. Frances Grymes,

Issue:

Hannah Philippa Ludwell, m. William Lee, above named,

Lucy Ludwell, m. John Paradise, by whom she had
a daughter, who m. Count Barzizi, a Venetian,
A daughter, Christian name unknown, appears to have died before
the date of her father's will, as she is not named therein, m.
William Edwards, second of that name in Virginia, who in his
will probated Feb. 21, 1721, directs Micajah Perry & Co. to pay
to his son Benjamin £100 sterling which Edwards had sent them,
and which had been bequeathed to said Benjamin by his grandfather Benjamin Harrison, Esq.,—The Councillor in his will gave
this amount to each grandchild except his eldest son's son,—
HENRY HARRISON, b. about 1693, member of the Council, d. s. p.
Sep. 24, 1732, "in the 40th year of his age," according to his tombstone at Cabin Point. His will, dated Sep. 11, 1732, recited in an
agreement of Oct. 27, 1732, left his plantation to his wife Elizabeth
for life, and then to his nephew Benjamin Harrison of Berkeley.
It tends to confirm the regicide tradition that the descendants of John
and Lucy Grymes (p. 49) have a tradition (see Meade) that their ancestor,
whose name apparently was not Grymes, was Lieutenant-General Thomas
——— of Cromwell's army. It is of course possible that Hannah, wife
of Harrison the Councillor, was daughter of Harrison the regicide.
Issue of Benjamin Harrison of Berkeley, who married Miss Carter:
  ANNE HARRISON, m. William Randolph of "Wilton,"
    Issue, appearing in Carter Family Tree:
      Peter Randolph,
      Peyton Randolph, m. his first cousin Lucy, dau. of Benja-
        min Harrison the Signer,
      Anne Randolph, d. s. p., m. (1st w. of) Benjamin Harrison
        of "Brandon,"
      Elizabeth Randolph, m. Philip Grymes,
      Lucy Randolph, m. Lewis Burwell,
  ELIZABETH HARRISON, d. s. p., m. Peyton Randolph, President
    of the first Continental Congress,
  BENJAMIN HARRISON, b. 1726, Signer of the Declaration of In-
    dependence, of whose descendants a complete account will appear
    in the work by Frank Willing Leach mentioned in the Intro-
    duction,—for the descendants of the Signer's son President Wil-
    liam Henry Harrison, see the Chart,—
  CARTER HENRY HARRISON, b. after Aug. 22, 1726, the date of
    Robert Carter's will which left to the second son of Benjamin
    and Anne (testator's daughter) Harrison, to be baptized Carter,
    in tail male, and in default to the third son in tail male, and in
    default to the eldest son in tail male, and in default to said
    Anne's heirs female, and in default of her issue male and female,
    then to testator's son Robert,—Carter Henry agreed to sell lands

entailed by Robert Carter's will, and an Act of Assembly was passed in 1761 docking the entail,—resided at "Clifton," Cumberland Co., and was a member of the Committee of Safety and of the House of Delegates, m. Susanna, dau. of Isham Randolph of "Dungeness,"

Issue:
- Robert Carter Harrison, b. June 14, 1765, removed to Kentucky about 1805, d. Sept. 9, 1840, m. Anne, dau. of Col. Joseph Cabell by his w. Mary Hopkins,
  - Issue among others:
    - Robert Carter Harrison, m. ——, dau. of William Russell of Fayette, Ky., and was father of Carter Henry Harrison, Mayor of Chicago,
    - Joseph Cabell Harrison (Rev.), of Boone and Kenton Counties, Ky.,
- Anne Harrison, m. Thomas Drew,
- Peyton Harrison, m. Elizabeth Barclay,
- Elizabeth Harrison, m. —— Bradley,
- Randolph Harrison, b. (Page's *Page Family*) Feb. 11, 1769, of "Clifton," m. Mch. 20, 1790, his cousin Mary, b. Feb. 1, 1773, dau. of Thomas Isham Randolph,
  - Issue, according to Page's *Page Family*, in which the remoter descendants are given:
    - Thomas Randolph Harrison, d. 1833, m. Eliza Cunningham,
    - Carter Henry Harrison, d. 1843, m. Janetta Fisher,
    - Archibald Morgan Harrison, d. 1842, m., 1st, Kitty Heth, and, 2nd, Fanny Taylor,
    - Jane Cary Harrison, d. 1883, m. William Fitzhugh Randolph,
    - Randolph Harrison, d. 1844, m. Heningham Carrington Wills,
    - Peyton Harrison (Rev.), of Baltimore, Md., m., 1st, Jane Carr, and, 2nd, Ellen M. Smith (see *Provincial Councillors of Pennsylvania, 1733–1776*),
    - William Mortimer Harrison, drowned in boyhood,
    - Mary Randolph Harrison, d. 1851, m. (1st w. of) William Byrd Harrison of "Upper Brandon,"
    - Susanna Isham Harrison, m. Rev. Samuel Blaine,
    - Lucia Cary Harrison, d. 1842, m. Nelson Page,
    - Catherine Lilbourne Harrison, m. John S. McKim of Baltimore,
    - Williana Mortimer Harrison, d. 1847, m. Henry Page Irving,

Virginia Randolph Harrison, d. y.,
Nannie Hartwell Harrison, m. John Bolling Garrett, M.D.,
Carter Henry Harrison, d. 1800,

HENRY HARRISON, recited in Act of Assembly as the third son, and as having died in infancy without issue,

CHARLES HARRISON, called the second child in the Carter Tree, Brig.-Gen. in Revolutionary War, d. 1796, m. Mary, dau. of Augustine Claiborne,
 Issue, according to *The Critic:*
  Charles Harrison,
  Augustine Harrison, d. inf.,
  Benjamin Harrison, b. June 30, 1775,
  Henry Harrison, twin with Benj.,
  Mary Herbert Harrison, m. John Herbert Peterson, see Browning's *Americans of Royal Descent,*
  Anne Carter Harrison, m. Matthew M. Claiborne,
  Elizabeth Randolph Harrison, m. Daniel Claiborne Butts,
  Susan Harrison, m. —— Withers,

NATHANIEL HARRISON, Speaker of State Senate, Sheriff of Prince George Co. in 1779, m., 1st, Anne, dau. of William Gilliam, and, 2nd, —— Ruffin,
 Issue, according to *The Critic*, which says by Anne Gilliam:
  Benjamin Harrison, m. —— Osborne, widow,
  John Harrison, d. y.,
  (a dau.) Harrison, m. —— Brown,
  Sarah Harrison, m. Donald McKenzie,
  (a dau.) Harrison, m. —— Boyd,
  Susan Harrison, m. Robert Maitland,
  Jane Harrison, m. John Osborne,

HENRY HARRISON,
 Issue:
  Henry Harrison, eldest son, said to have d. s. p., and to have had a sister who m. —— Cocke,

ROBERT HARRISON, of Charles City Co., d. before 1771, m. —— Collier,
 Issue:
  Collier Harrison, eldest son, d. Nov., 1809,
  Braxton Harrison,
  perhaps others,
two daughters killed by lightning with their father.

IRWIN.

THERE is a tradition, which I have not succeeded in verifying, that the Irwin family in the Chart were descended from the John Irwin who received a manor in Ireland in Cromwell's time.

Archibald Irwin, the great-great-grandfather of President Benjamin Harrison, appears to have been born in that country. Mrs. Newcomer of Indianapolis, among other information kindly furnished me, tells me that this Archibald settled where his son and grandson of the same name afterwards resided, four miles south of the site of Mercersburg, Franklin County, Pa. This was formerly in Peters Township, Cumberland County, and a list of owners of land in that Township in 1763 mentions an Archibald Irwin with two hundred acres, for which the warrants had already been issued, twenty acres being cleared, and nine sown, and with two horses and two cows. John, James, William, and another John appear in the same list, each having more acres cleared than Archibald. It is probable that this first Archibald, rather than his son, was the Ensign Archibald Irwin of the Rev. John Steel's company of Armstrong's battalion in 1756, during the French and Indian War.

The first Archibald had issue, the order of birth being uncertain:
JOSEPH IRWIN, m. Violet Porter,
JAMES IRWIN,
ARCHIBALD IRWIN, m. Jean McDowell, see below,
JOHN IRWIN, m. —— Hage,
MARY IRWIN, m. —— Nesbith,
JANE IRWIN, m. John Boggs,
LYDIA IRWIN, m. Moses Porter,
MARTHA IRWIN, m. George Paull,
daughter, m. —— McConnell,
daughter, m. —— McConnell.

ARCHIBALD IRWIN, great-grandfather of President Benjamin Harrison, was probably born in Ireland. During the Revolutionary War, he was Quartermaster of Col. Samuel Culbertson's battalion of Cumberland County militia. This Archibald built a fine stone dwelling-house, and operated a flour-mill and saw-mill, whence the place came to be called "Irwinton Mills." He is sometimes styled "merchant" in the records. He was an elder of the Presbyterian Church at Mercersburg. He died of palsy in the Winter of 1798–9.

Issue:
> JAMES IRWIN, b. Apr. 14, 1758, m. Margaret Smith, see below,
> MARY IRWIN, b. Feb. 14, 1760, m. M. Van Lear, see p. 57,
> MARGARET IRWIN, b. Sep. 10, 1761, d. unm.,
> NANCY IRWIN, b. Apr. 27, 1763, m. Wm. Findlay, see p. 58,
> WILLIAM IRWIN, b. Feb. 5, 1766, m. Mary Smith, see p. 60,
> ELIZABETH IRWIN, b. Aug. 24, 1767, m. Robert Smith, see p. 62,
> JANE IRWIN, b. June 22, 1769, resided with her niece at the White House (p. 65), d. s. p. Dec. 28, 1850, m. James Findlay, brother of Governor Findlay, and Colonel in War of 1812, General, Member of Congress from 1825 to 1833, Democratic candidate for Governor of Ohio in 1834, d. Cincinnati Dec. 28, 1835,
> ARCHIBALD IRWIN, b. Feb. 13, 1772, m., 1st, Mary Ramsey, and, 2nd, Sidney Grubb, see p. 64,
> JOHN IRWIN, b. Mch. 4, 1773, drowned while a child.

JAMES IRWIN, b. in York Co., Pa., Apr. 14, 1758, eldest son of Archibald, as above, enlisted in the Revolutionary War first as a private, and from 1778 to 1781 was Assistant Commissary for the Western Army. His father left his brother William and himself a farm in Peters Township. He died in Cincinnati, while on a visit there, Nov. 9, 1843, m. Dec. 5, 1787, his first cousin Margaret, widow of William Smith, and daughter of William Piper by his w. Sarah McDowell (see notes on McDowell family).
Issue :
> ARCHIBALD IRWIN, b. Oct. 9, 1788, d. May 31, 1797,
> MARY SMITH IRWIN, b. Jany. 6, 1790, m. James McClelland, see below,
> WILLIAM IRWIN, b. Nov. 24, 1791, m. Ann Hamilton, see p. 55,
> JOHN IRWIN, b. Feb. 1, 1794, d. unm. Oct. 13, 1838,
> JAMES IRWIN, b. Mch. 28, 1797, d. March 4, 1798,
> ARCHIBALD JAMES IRWIN, b. Dec. 15, 1798, d. s. p. St. Louis, Nov. 14, 1867, m. Mary Stuart Hunton, dau. of Charles Hunton,
> MATTHEW IRWIN, b. Sep. 5, 1800, m. Florence McL. Wilson, see p. 56,
> JANE F. IRWIN, b. June 30, 1803, d. unm. Apr. 12, 1852.

MARY SMITH IRWIN, b. Jany. 6, 1790, daughter of James Irwin, above named, d. June, 1863, m. Jany. 26, 1814, James McClelland of Franklin County, Pa., b. July, 1776, d. Mch., 1863.
Issue :
> John McClelland, d. unm. in Florida,
> James Irwin McClelland, b. Sep., 1816, d. Huntsville, Ala., May 12, 1855, m. Eliza, d. Dec. 17, 1885, dau. of John Eakin from County Derry, Ireland,

Issue:
>   Willie S. McClelland, d. unm. Jany. 31, 1866,
>   Mary Irwin McClelland, of Shelbyville, Tenn., unm.,
>
> Sidney McClelland, d. s. p., m. her mother's first cousin Matthew S. Van Lear (p. 57),
>
> William Archibald McClelland, of St. Louis, m. Louisa Morris Edgar, d. Nov. 13, 1888, dau. of Rev. J. T. Edgar, D.D., Pastor of First Presbyterian Church, Nashville, Tenn., Moderator of General Assembly of 1842,
>
> Issue:
> >   Edgar McClelland, of St. Louis, unm.,
> >   Mary McClelland, unm.,
> >   Margaret Irwin McClelland, unm.,
> >   William Archibald McClelland, d. unm.,
> >   James Irwin McClelland, unm.,
> >   Joseph Van Lear McClelland, unm.,
> >   Thomas Wharton McClelland, unm.,
> >   Frank Morris McClelland, unm.,
>
> Joseph Grubb McClelland, d. unm. in Missouri, 1876,
>
> Matthew Van Lear McClelland, of Wellington, Mo., m. Sarah Elizabeth Bay, dau. of Samuel Mansfield Bay,
>
> Issue:
> >   Mansfield Bay McClelland, unm.,
> >   Mary Irwin McClelland, unm.,
> >   Virginia McClelland, unm.,
> >   James McClelland, unm.,
> >   Sarah Bay McClelland, unm.
>
> Margaret Irwin McClelland, of Mercersburg, Pa., unm.

WILLIAM IRWIN, b. Nov. 24, 1791, son of James Irwin, p. 54, d. Mch. 5, 1847, m. Ann Hamilton.

Issue:
>   James Irwin, d. 1859, m. Margaret Elizabeth, d. 1887, dau. of Henry Kulp by his w. Sarah Beck,
>
>   Issue:
>   >   William Irwin, cashier of Nat. Bank of Mifflin Co., Lewistown,
>   >   Margaret James Irwin, d. unm. 1880,
>   >   Anne Irwin, of Lewistown, unm.,
>   >   Sarah Beck Irwin, of Lewistown, unm.,
>
>   John Irwin, d. 1890, m. Sarah Harrison,
>
>   Issue:
>   >   Anna Mary Irwin, m. Rev. Charles Lippincott,
>   >
>   >   Issue:
>   >   >   John Irwin Lippincott,
>
>   William Irwin, d. Oct., 1892,
>
>   Sarah Irwin, d. 1882, m. Abram Warder, M.D., d. 1890,
>
>   Issue:
>   >   Virginia Warder, d. s. p., m. H. Comerford,
>   >   Abram Warder, M.D., unm.,
>   >   Mary Warder, m. Marmaduke Dent, Judge of Supreme Court,

Issue:
    Marmaduke Dent,
    Caroline Dent,
    John Irwin Warder, m. Ida, dau. of —— Branen, Judge,
    Issue:
        John Irwin Warder,
        Henry Branen Warder,
        Ida Jackson Warder,
Margaret Irwin, of Clarksburg, W. Va., unm.,
Mary Irwin, of Clarksburg, unm.,
Anna Irwin, of Clarksburg, unm.,
Eliza Irwin, m., 1st, —— Smith, and, 2nd, —— Lee,
    Issue:
        unknown.

MATTHEW IRWIN, b. Sep. 5, 1800, son of James Irwin, p. 54, d. 1872, m. Jany. 15, 1846, Florence McLean Wilson, b. Jany. 6, 1820, dau. of David Wilson by his w. Martha Agnew, and granddau. of David Wilson of Gettysburg by his w. Jane Rowan (see Nevin's *Presbyterian Encyclopædia*).
Issue:
    Margaret Irwin, b. Nov. 12, 1846, m. Nov. 16, 1869, Joseph W. Winger,
        Issue:
            Matthew Irwin Winger, b. Nov. 15, 1870,
            Josephine Weaver Winger, b. Sep. 28, 1872,
            Florence McLean Winger, b. Jany. 7, 1874,
            James Wilson Winger, b. Feb. 14, 1875,
            Ralph Oberlin Winger, b. Sep. 16, 1877,
            Margaret Irwin Winger, b. Sep. 16, 1879,
    Mary McClelland Irwin, b. Sep. 25, 1848, m. Sep. 10, 1872, Thomas A. Creigh, now of Omaha, son of Rev. Thomas Creigh, D.D., of Mercersburg, by his w. Jane McClelland Grubb (sister of Archibald Irwin's 2nd w. Sidney Grubb),
        Issue:
            Thomas Creigh, b. Aug. 8, 1873,
            Alfred Irwin Creigh, b. Mch. 14, 1884,
    Elizabeth Wilson Irwin, b. Aug. 2, 1850, unm.,
    Emiline Van Lear Irwin, b. May 23, 1853, m. Oct. 4, 1876, Thomas Harrison McGahey, now of Lincoln, Neb.,
        Issue:
            Mary Wilson McGahey, b. July 26, 1877,
            Florence Irwin McGahey, b. June 4, 1880,
            (infant son) McGahey, b. June 4, 1880, d. June 7, 1880,
            Aleck McGahey, b. Mch. 11, 1883, d. Aug. 9, 1883,
            Donald McGahey, b. Oct. 30, 1885, d. Mch., 1887,
            Jean Elizabeth McGahey, b. 1891,
    James McClelland Irwin, b. Mch. 2, 1855, of Quincy, Ill., m. Oct. 10, 1883, Carrie, b. Dec. 17, 1858, dau. of Burr H. Polk by his w. Eliza Anne Montgomery,

Issue:
  Annie Montgomery Irwin, b. Sep. 13, 1884, d. Aug. 18, 1885,
  Burr Polk Irwin, b. Dec. 25, 1885,
  James Matthew Irwin, b. Mch. 7, 1889,
Ada Jane Irwin, b. Aug. 14, 1857, m. in 1881 Thomas M. Atkinson, d. Oct., 1886,
  Issue:
    Sidney Atkinson, b. Aug. 22, 1882,
    Florence Wilson Atkinson, b. Mch. 28, 1884, d. Feb., 1886,
    Rachel Atkinson, b. Mch. 1, 1887.

MARY IRWIN, b. Feb. 14, 1760, daughter of Archibald Irwin, p. 54, d. June 28, 1828, m. Matthew Van Lear, son of John Van Lear. Matthew Van Lear, after some years of mercantile life, resided at a plantation called "Mount Tammany," near Williamsport, Md., still in the possession of the family. He died July 5, 1823, in his sixty-eighth year.
  Issue:
  JANE VAN LEAR, b. Feb. 16, 1784, d. Mch. 26, 1828, m. John Ramsey, see the account of the Ramsey family,
  JOHN VAN LEAR, b. Nov. 18, 1786, merchant in Baltimore, afterwards President of Bank of Washington County, Md., d. unm. April 24, 1857,
  —— VAN LEAR, b. Feb. 9, 1790, d. (only issue of one Mrs. Finley was a dau. who d. y., the other Mrs. Finley d. s. p.), m. John Finley, merchant in Baltimore,
  —— VAN LEAR, b. Feb. 9, 1790, d. (see statement as to her twin sister), m. Michael A. Finley, M.D., practised in Williamsport, Md., d. Mch. 25, 1848, aged sixty-two,
  WILLIAM VAN LEAR, b. Jany. 29, 1794, m. Susan Graham, see below,
  MATTHEW SIMS VAN LEAR, b. July 8, 1795, d. s. p. Dec. 19, 1852, m. Sidney McClelland, dau. of his first cousin (p. 55),
  JAMES VAN LEAR, b. Dec. 16, 1796, d. unm. July 20, 1820,
  HORATIO NELSON VAN LEAR, b. Sep. 6, 1798, d. unm. Aug. 20, 1823,
  JOSEPH VAN LEAR, b. Apr. 10, 1800, d. unm. Oct. 21, 1859,
  SOPHIA VAN LEAR, b. Feb. 12, 1804, d. Apr. 21, 1881, m. her cousin Archibald Irwin Findlay, see p. 58,
  two others, there having been twelve in all.

WILLIAM VAN LEAR, b. Jany. 29, 1794, A.B. and M.D. (Jeff.), practised medicine at Williamsport, Md., d. May, 1837, m. Susan Graham, b. near Bedford, Pa., in 1800, d. Dec., 1855.
  Issue:
  James Van Lear, d. y.,

William Van Lear, b. 1823, lawyer, d. unm. Cumberland, Md., in 1853,

Mary Irwin Van Lear, b. 1826, d. 1860, m. 1855 her cousin Casper Shunk, son of Governor Shunk by his w. Jane Findlay, see p. 60,

Edward Williams Van Lear, d. y.,

John Horace Van Lear, Major, now of Hagerstown, Md., m. his cousin Mary, dau. of John King Findlay (p. 59),
> Issue:
> Susan Van Lear, d. y.,
> John Findlay Van Lear,
> William Van Lear,

Matthew Van Lear, d. inf.,

child, d. inf.,

Matthew Van Lear, b. Apr 10, 1837, A.B. (Princeton), Pastor of Presbyterian Church at Winchester, Ky., and now at Shreveport, La., m. Isabella, dau. of Thomas Chalkley Atkinson of Alexandria, Va.,
> Issue:
> Isabella Van Lear,
> Susan Graham Van Lear, m. W. H. Morton, Professor in charge of Potomac Seminary, Romney, W. Va.,
>> Issue:
>> Isabella Morton,
> Anna Croxall Van Lear,
> John Van Lear, theological student,
> Thomas Atkinson Van Lear,
> Matthew Van Lear,
> William Van Lear,
> Mary Ellen Van Lear.

NANCY IRWIN, b. Apr. 27, 1763, daughter of Archibald Irwin, p. 54, called "Agnes" in her father's will, d. July 27, 1824, m., acc. to Armor's *Lives of the Governors of Pennsylvania*, Dec. 7, 1791, William Findlay, b. Mercersburg, June 20, 1768, Governor of Pennsylvania, and United States Senator, d. Harrisburg, Nov. 12, 1846.
> Issue:
> SAMUEL FINDLAY, lawyer in Cincinnati, d. unm.,
> JAMES FINDLAY, lawyer at Greensburg, and afterwards in Pittsburgh, Secretary of the Commonwealth of Pennsylvania under Governor Wolf from 1833 to 1835, d. unm. in Pittsburgh before the death of his law partner, Governor Shunk,
> ARCHIBALD IRWIN FINDLAY, b. Jany. 21, 1799, practised law in Chambersburg, Pa., d. Oct. 8, 1839, m. Oct., 1829, his first cousin Sophia Van Lear (see p. 57),
>> Issue:
>> Nancy Irwin Findlay, b. Sep. 28, 1831, of "Mount Tammany," unm.,

James Irwin Findlay, b. Sep. 30, 1837, of "Mount Tammany," unm.,
John Van Lear Findlay, b. Dec. 21, 1839, A.B. (Princeton), lawyer in Baltimore, City Solicitor, Member of Congress from 1883 to 1887, umpire on Venezuelan Claims Commission, m., 1st, Mary C., dau. of J. P. Mackenzie, M.D., of Baltimore, and, 2nd, Mary, dau. of V. K. Keesey of York, Pa.,
  Issue by 1st wife:
    one child, d. y.,
  Issue by 2nd wife:
    Mary V. L. Findlay,
    V. K. Findlay,
JANE FINDLAY, m. Francis R. Shunk, see below,
JOHN KING FINDLAY, b. near Mercersburg, May 12, 1803, grad. at West Point, asst. professor there, lawyer and Judge in Philadelphia, Presiding Judge of Dist. Court embracing Northampton County, Pa., after middle age a magistrate of Philadelphia, d. at Spring Lake, N.J., Sep. 13, 1885, m., 1st, Susan Ogelsby of Hagerstown, and, 2nd, Sibilla S. Kennedy née Morris,—by her Judge Findlay had no issue,—
  Issue by 1st wife:
    William Findlay, d. y.,
    Mary Irwin Findlay, m. her second cousin John H. Van Lear, see p. 58,
ROBERT SMITH FINDLAY, d. unm.

JANE FINDLAY, above named, daughter of William Findlay, the Governor, and Nancy Irwin his wife, d. 1878, m. Francis Rawn Shunk, Governor of Pennsylvania, who d. Harrisburg, July 30, 1848.
  Issue:
    Francis J. Shunk, Major U.S.A., d. s. p. Dec. 15, 1867,
    William Findlay Shunk, now Chief Engineer of Inter-Continental Railroad, m. Gertrude, dau. of John Wyeth of Harrisburg, by his w. Elmira Canfield,
      Issue:
        Jane Findlay Shunk, d. inf.,
        Nelly Findlay Shunk,
        Mary Douglas Shunk,
        Gertrude Wyeth Shunk, dec'd, m. James Parker of Perth Amboy, N.J.,
          Issue:
            James Parker,
        Nancy Irwin Shunk,
        Francis Rawn Shunk, grad. at head of his class at West Point, now 1st Lieut. U. S. Engineers,
        Elizabeth Brown Shunk, m. John Alexander Harman, 2nd Lieut. U. S. Cavalry,

Issue:
    Gertrude Harman,
    Archer Harman,
Caspar Shunk, of Williamsport, Md., m. Jany., 1855, his second cousin Mary Irwin Van Lear (p. 58),
  Issue:
    Mary Van Lear Shunk, m. Robert Braden Wright,
    Issue:
      Robert Van Lear Wright,
      Edith Wright,
Nancy Findlay Shunk, m. (2nd w. of) Henry Chapman, Judge, of Bucks County, Pa.,
  Issue:
    Frances Chapman, of Doylestown, Pa., unm.,
    Arthur Chapman, of Doylestown, unm.,
Elizabeth Rawn Shunk, d. 1865, m. Charles Brown of Philadelphia, Collector of the Port, who d. 1883,
  Issue:
    Elizabeth Shunk Brown, m. P. S. Downs, M.D., of Kent County, Del.,
    Issue:
      Charles Brown Downs,
      Nellie Findlay Downs,
      Francis Shunk Downs,
      William Findlay Downs,
      Donald Irwin Downs,
    Charles Brown, dec'd,
    Annie Brown, d. y.,
    Jane Findlay Brown, dec'd, m Zadoc H. Postles of Kent County, Del.,
    Issue:
      Helen Jeans Postles,
      Lillie Shunk Postles,
      Elizabeth Brown Postles,
      Findlay Postles,
    Francis Shunk Brown, of Phila. bar, m. Elizabeth, dau. of Pleasanton Hamm of Kent County, Del.,
    Issue:
      Francis Shunk Brown,
    William Findlay Brown, of Phila. bar, m. Julia Schoonmacker, dau. of Rev. A. A. Willetts, D.D., of Louisville, Ky.,
    Issue:
      William Findlay Brown,
      Alexander Paul Brown,
    Lillie Brown, m. William McGonigal Jr. of Matthews County, Va.,
    Alexander Miller Brown, m. Fannie Reynolds of Newcastle County, Del.

WILLIAM IRWIN, b. Feb. 5, 1766, son of Archibald, see p. 54, removed to Cincinnati, d. July 16, 1824, m. Mary, dau. of Robert Smith by his w. Grizzela Newall.
  Issue:
    ARCHIBALD IRWIN, b. Sep. 20, 1796, of Cincinnati, d. Sep. 4, 1852, m. Emily Albino, dau. of George W. Jones of Cincinnati,
    Issue:

Mary Jane Irwin, d. unm.,
Esther Allibone Irwin, d. June 8, 1891, m. 1863 (2nd w. of) William Carson, M.D., of Cincinnati, descended from James Claypoole of Phila., who was brother of Oliver Cromwell's son-in-law (see Browning's *Americans of Royal Descent*),
> Issue:
> Archibald Irwin Carson, M.D., of Cincinnati, unm.,
> Mary Claypoole Carson, unm.,

Louisa Irwin, d. unm.,
William Sloo Irwin, dec'd, m. Lily Graham,
> Issue:
> William Irwin, d. unm.,
> Archibald Irwin, d. unm.,

Sarah Eliza Irwin, m. Ebenezer Gay,
> Issue:
> Lulu Gay, unm.,

Emily Irwin, d. unm.,
George Augustus Irwin, d. unm.,
Archibald Irwin, d. unm.,

JANE IRWIN, d. unm.,
HARRIET IRWIN, dec'd, m. (1st w. of) Thomas Sloo, who afterwards m. Rebecca Findlay,
Issue:
William Irwin Sloo, d. unm.,

LOUISA IRWIN, dec'd, m. (1st w. of) Lewis Whiteman,
Issue:
Harriet Irwin Whiteman, m. her cousin William F. Irwin, see p. 65,
William Irwin Whiteman, d. St. Paul, Minn., Mch. 24, 1863, m. Frances, d. Cincinnati, Feb. 15, 1879, dau. of James Hall, Judge, a grandson of Provost Ewing of Univ. of Penna.,
> Issue:
> Louisa Irwin Whiteman, m. Rev. James Sydney Kent, Rector of St. Mary's Church, Ardmore, Pa., d. Aug. 14, 1890, s. of Wm. Kent of Montreal,
>> Issue:
>> Frances Hall Kent,
>> Mary Elizabeth Kent,
>> Margaret Yseult Kent,
>> Dorothea Kent,
>
> James Hall Whiteman, of Seattle, m. Nannie, dau. of Jacob B. Braden of St. Paul, Minn., no issue,
> Mary Posey Whiteman, of New York, unm.,
> William Lewis Whiteman, of Port Angelus, Wash.,

Louisa Jane Findlay Whiteman, d. 1859, m. 1854 (1st w. of) William Carson, M.D.,

Issue:
> Jane Findlay Carson, unm.,
> Eliza Carson, m. James Faran,
> Issue:
>> Jane Findlay Faran,
>> James John Faran,
> Lewis Whiteman Carson, d. y.,

WILLIAM IRWIN, b. Jany. 30, 1806, of Cincinnati, dec'd, m., 1st, Mary Jane Smith, who d. s. p., and he m., 2nd, July 31, 1838, Sarah Louisa, dau. of John Ramsey by his w. Jane Van Lear (see Ramsey),
> Issue by 2nd wife:
> Jane Van Lear Irwin, d. y.,
> John Ramsey Irwin, d. y.,
> William Harmar Irwin, d. y.,
> Mary Irwin, d. y.,
> Joseph Van Lear Irwin, of Wakeeney, Kan., unm.,
> Fannie Ramsey Irwin, d. y.,
> Sallie Irwin, d. y.,

JAMES FINDLAY IRWIN, b. Apr. 11, 1808, d. Nov. 21, 1872, m. Mch. 20, 1833, Lydia Ridgely Gassaway, b. June 21, 1811, d. Sep. 18, 1883, dau. of Henry Gassaway by his w. Rachel Griffith,
> Issue:
> William Irwin, d. y.,
> Louise Whiteman Irwin, of Philadelphia, unm.,
> Henry Gassaway Irwin, d. unm., Galveston, May 11, 1882,
> James Findlay Irwin, in Union Army, d. Mch. 13, 1865,
> Elizabeth Griffith Irwin, d. y. Feb. 26, 1864,
> Mary Irwin, d. y. June 10, 1862,
> John Van Lear Irwin, d. y. Oct. 17, 1866.

ELIZABETH IRWIN, b. Aug. 24, 1767, dau. of Archibald, p. 54, d. Mch. 20, 1814, m. Robert Smith, Speaker of House of Rep. of Penna., State Senator, and an Associate Judge, d. Apr. 21, 1849, aged eighty-three. He was uncle of Gov. Findlay and Gen. Findlay, both of whom, moreover, married sisters of his wife.
> Issue:
> JANE IRWIN SMITH, b. Apr. 30, 1792, d. at Chambersburg, Sep. 29, 1827, m. Apr. 7, 1815, Alexander Tracy Dean, M.D., of Chambersburg, s. of Alexander Dean by his w. Anna Adams,
>> Issue:
>> Elizabeth S. Dean, b. Apr. 22, 1816, d. Sep. 7, 1817,
>> Anna Mary Dean, b. Aug. 20, 1819, d. 1845, m. William Young, M.D., afterwards of Mt. Vernon, Ind.,—his mother

was Mary Irwin, a first cousin of Elizabeth, w. of Robert Smith,—
Issue:
William Young, d. inf.,
Alexander Dean Young, d. inf.,
Anna Mary Young, of Phila., unm.,
Robert Smith Dean, b. Feb. 1, 1822, lawyer of Cincinnati, d. s. p. in New Orleans, Oct., 1867, m., July, 1853, —— Baltzell of Baltimore,

WILLIAM SMITH, b. Dec. 26, 1796, of Mercersburg, a soldier of the War of 1812, Captain, d. Oct. 15, 1846, m., Nov. 4, 1818, Mary Smith Johnston, dau. of John Johnston, soldier of the Revolution, Captain, by his 2nd w. Annabella,
Issue:
Elizabeth Irwin Smith, b. Sep. 2, 1820, now of Gettysburg, Pa., m., Oct. 23, 1844, John S. Crawford,
Issue:
William H. Crawford, served in Union Army, m. Gertrude, dau. of Galbraith Irvine, M.D., of Warren, Pa.,
Issue:
Anne Elizabeth Crawford, m. James Martindale Hawxhurst of Chicago, no issue,
Mary Johnston Crawford, m. John Morris Krauth of Gettysburg, dec'd,
Issue:
Harriet Krauth,
Elizabeth Krauth,
Robert Smith Crawford, of Hagerstown, Md., m. Lucy Lothrop of Boston,
Issue:
Annie Lothrop Crawford,
Ruth Sybilla Crawford,
George Douglas Crawford, of Washington, D.C., m. Lilla Reeves, dau. of Mark and Eliza A. Reeves of Washington,
Issue:
Blanche Crawford,
Mary Reeves Crawford,
Anna Bella Smith, d. at Greensburg, Pa., m. Rev. Samuel H. Giesy, dec'd,
Issue:
Harry Giesy, dec'd,
Anne Giesy, dec'd,
William J. Smith, of Woodburn, Iowa, d. Feb. 28, 1875, m. Rebecca M., dau. of Samuel Johnston Work,
Issue:
William Work Smith, d. s. p.,
Mary Rebekah Smith, d. s. p.,
Anna Lizzie Smith, d. s. p.,
Samuel Johnston Smith, d. s. p.,
Jane Smith, of Chicago, unm.,

SARAH SMITH, b. Oct. 10, 1803, d. Mercersburg, Dec. 9, 1856, m. Nov. 24, 1824, John Findlay, nephew of Gov. Findlay, and s. of Col. John Findlay of Chambersburg, who was a Member of Congress (see notes on McDowell),

Issue:
  Elizabeth Findlay, b. Sep. 8, 1825, now of Boone, Iowa, m. Dec. 21, 1852, Perry A. Rice, lawyer and justice of the peace, who d. in Libby Prison Feb. 27, 1863,

  Issue:
    John Findlay Rice, of Ouray, Colorado, m. Grace M., dau. of Justin Ayres of Osceola, Iowa,
    Issue:
      Frank Ayres Rice,
      Elizabeth Findlay Rice,
    Thomas Williard Rice, d. inf.,
    Robert Smith Findlay Rice, of Osceola, Iowa, m. Ella, dau. of Wm. Farson of Dresden, Ohio,
    Issue:
      William Perry Rice,
      Sara Findlay Rice, Principal of High School at Boone, Iowa, unm.,
    William Perry Rice, b. Apr. 21, 1863, d. unm. Aug. 24, 1887,
  son, unnamed, b. Apr. 8, 1827, d. inf.,
  John Findlay, b. May 26, 1828, d. Dec. 29, 1832,
  Robert Smith Findlay, b. Mch. 29, 1832, served in Union Army, now of Osceola, Iowa, m. Sep. 14, 1876, Emma, dau. of James Lash of Mt. Pleasant, Iowa,
  Issue:
    John Torrence Findlay,
    William Perry Findlay, d. 1879,
    Elizabeth Rice Findlay,
    James Lash Findlay, d. 1883,
    Emma Lash Findlay,
    Anna Mary Findlay,
    Robert Smith Findlay,
    Grace Rice Findlay.

ARCHIBALD IRWIN, b. Feb. 13, 1772, s. of Archibald Irwin, p. 54, was baptized on Mch. 2 by Rev. John King, D.D., Pastor of Mercersburg Church, and d. of apoplexy, Mch. 3, 1840, m., 1st, Oct. 11, 1798, "Polly Ramsay," as the Church record calls her, i.e. Mary, dau. of James Ramsey (see account of the Ramsey family), she d. Feb. 10, 1813, and, 2nd, Dec. 15, 1813, Sidney Grubb, b. near Mercersburg, Mch. 9, 1789, d. Mch. 31, 1869, dau. of Joseph Grubb by his w. Jane McClelland, Joseph Grubb being son of Thomas Grubb of Lancaster County by his w. Isabella Polk, and grandson of Emanuel Grubb, who came from Cornwall, England.

Issue by 1st wife:
  JAMES RAMSEY IRWIN, b. Dec. 1, 1800, grad. West Point, became Capt. U.S.A. in 1844, served in Mexican War, Chief Quarter-

master of Gen. Scott's army, d. s. p. in City of Mexico during its occupation, Jany. 10, 1848,

JANE IRWIN, b. July 23, 1804, brought up in Cincinnati by her aunt Mrs. James Findlay, presided at the White House during the elder President Harrison's short term, d. May 11, 1846, m., 1st, William Henry Harrison, b. Sep. 26, 1802, grad. Transylvania Univ., practised law in Cincinnati, d. Feb. 6, 1838, s. of President William Henry Harrison, and she m., 2nd, Lewis Whiteman of Cincinnati, but by the latter had no issue,

Issue by 1st husband:
See the Chart,

JOHN RAMSEY IRWIN, b. May 22, 1807, d. s. p., m. Anna Eaton,
ARCHIBALD IRWIN, twin with John Ramsey Irwin, d. s. p. Sep., 1852, m. Martha Sumwault,
ELIZABETH IRWIN, b. July 18, 1810, d. Aug. 15, 1850, m. Aug. 12, 1831, (2nd w. of) John Scott Harrison, b. Oct. 4, 1804, farmer at North Bend, Member of Congress, d. May, 1878, s. of President William Henry Harrison,

Issue:
Benjamin Harrison, President, and others, see the Chart,
Issue by 2nd wife:
JOSEPH GRUBB IRWIN, b. Oct. 10, 1814, d. unm.,
WILLIAM FINDLAY IRWIN, b. July 18, 1817, now of Cincinnati, m. Oct. 12, 1848, his cousin Harriet Irwin Whiteman (p. 61),
Issue:
Lewis Whiteman Irwin, of Cincinnati, m. Alice Key Dandridge, dau. of Dr. Alexander Spotswood Dandridge of Cincinnati, no issue,
Archibald Irwin, d. unm.,
Louisa Irwin, unm.,
Jane Findlay Irwin, unm.,
MARY JANE IRWIN, b. Oct. 16, 1819, d. unm. Dec. 21, 1838,
NANCY ISABELLA IRWIN, b. Apr. 9, 1822, d. Feb. 12, 1845, m. Cephas B. Huston, now of Indianapolis,
Issue:
Mary Huston, m. Ira Harris, now of West Superior, Wisconsin, son of Ira Harris of Albany, N. Y., United States Senator,
Issue:
Louise H. Harris,
Ira Harris,
Jane Whiteman Huston, m. Rev. John Dixon of Trenton, N.J.,
Issue:
Huston Dixon,
Marion Dixon,

LOUISA IRWIN, b. July 15, 1824, m. Charles B. Maclay, M.D., of Peoria, Ill.,
  Issue:
    Sidney Maclay, m. Charles Booth,
      Issue:
        Louisa Booth,
        Maclay Booth,
    John Maclay, m. Ray Irwin,
      Issue:
        Dorothy Maclay,
    Archibald Maclay, m. Josephine Horton,
      Issue:
        Josephine Horton,
    Harriet Maclay, m. Eugene Fisher,
      Issue:
        Louisa Fisher,
        Janet Fisher,
        Eleanor Fisher,
        Anna Fisher,
    Hannah Maclay, d. s. p.,
    Louisa Maclay, unm.,
    Charles Maclay, d. s. p.,
SARAH ELLEN IRWIN, b. July 15, 1828, of Indianapolis, m. Frisby Snively Newcomer, M.D., d. 1889, a native of Hagerstown, Md.,
  Issue:
    Mary Newcomer, m. Benjamin Doolittle Walcott, s. of Wm. D. Walcott of New York mills,
      Issue:
        Harris Walcott,
        Gladys Walcott,
        Nancy Walcott,
    George Mears Newcomer, of New York, m. Alice, dau. of William Vincent Kay of Chicago, by his w. Jane Gibson,
      Issue:
        Marjorie Newcomer,
        Martin Newcomer,
        Vincent Kay Newcomer,
    Nancy Irwin Newcomer, unm.,
SIDNEY GRUBB IRWIN, b. Feb. 20, 1833, d. Jany. 10, 1865, m. John Grubb,
  Issue:
    William Irwin Grubb, of Birmingham, Ala., unm.

McDOWELL.

ACCORDING to tradition communicated to me by William H. McDowell of Chambersburg, Pa., William McDowell, his great-grandfather, was born in Scotland, and went to the North of Ireland during the time of religious persecution. As he was in his infancy when the persecution of the Presbyterians took place, he must have been taken to Ireland by his father, and the latter must have been the person who sought an asylum. William McDowell, if, indeed, he was not born in that country, certainly married there, and had three or four children before coming to America. He and his family came over about 1718, and settled in Chester County, Pennsylvania, where they remained until the fall of 1730 or spring of 1731, and then removed to the foot of Parnell's Knob, about ten miles west of Chambersburg. They were driven away by the invasion of the Indians, following Braddock's defeat. William McDowell died in 1757, aged about seventy-seven, near the present town of Wrightsville, York County, and was buried at the Presbyterian Church at Donegal, Lancaster County.

Issue:

JOHN McDOWELL, b. about 1715, m. Agnes ———, see below,
WILLIAM McDOWELL, b. about 1720, m. Mary Maxwell, see p. 70,
NATHAN McDOWELL,
JAMES McDOWELL,
THOMAS McDOWELL,
SARAH McDOWELL, m. William Piper, see p. 71,
JEAN McDOWELL, m. Archibald Irwin, see account of the Irwin family,
(dau.) McDOWELL, m. ——— Newell of Franklin Co.,
(dau.) McDOWELL, m. ——— Reynolds of Franklin Co.

JOHN McDOWELL, above mentioned, built a mill, which was the site of a fort called McDowell's in the French and Indian War, d. June 6, 1794, aged seventy-eight, m. Agnes, d. Aug. 8, 1766, aged fifty-one.

Issue, order uncertain:

MARY McDOWELL, m. Richard Brownson, see next page,
AGNES McDOWELL, b. Sep. 9, 1740, d. June 9, 1790, m. Mch. 19, 1771, Elias Davidson, b. 1736, of Antrim Township, Franklin Co., d. Apr. 15, 1806 (these dates taken from *History of Franklin County*, and have not been verified),
Issue:

JOHN MCDOWELL DAVIDSON, b. Jany. 4, 1772, d. Jany. 5, 1811, m., 1st, —— Maxwell, and, 2nd, Mary McLaughlin, who d. Jany. 28, 1851,
  Issue by 1st wife:
    several,
  Issue by 2nd wife:
    James King Davidson, M.D., for some years President of Greencastle Bank,
ELIZABETH MCDOWELL, said to have been the third daughter, m. June, 1768, Rev. John King, D.D., Pastor of Upper West Conococheague (afterwards Mercersburg) Church, b. Dec. 5, 1740, son of Robert King, and Moderator of the General Assembly of the Presbyterian Church of 1792, d. July 15, 1813,
  (dau.) McDOWELL, m. George King.

MARY MCDOWELL, see preceding page, m. Richard Brownson, M.D., nephew of Dr. Nathan Brownson, Governor of Georgia. Dr. Richard Brownson was surgeon in the Revolutionary Army.
  Issue:
    NANCY BROWNSON, m. John Findlay, see below,
    JOHN BROWNSON, m. Sarah Smith, see p. 69,
    ELIZABETH BROWNSON, d. unm.,
    ABIGAIL BROWNSON, d. unm.,
    NATHAN BROWNSON, d. unm.,
    TIMOTHY BROWNSON, d. y.,
    ASA BROWNSON, d. unm.

NANCY BROWNSON, above named, m. (1st w. of) John Findlay, b. 1766, of Chambersburg, Colonel and Member of Congress, brother of Governor William Findlay, and son of Samuel Findlay by his w. Jane Smith.
  Issue:
    Jane Findlay, d. Apr. 27, 1827, m., May 6, 1819, John Maclay,
      Issue:
        William Irwin Maclay, b. Mch. 27, 1820, dec'd, m. Sarah H. Stackhouse,
        Issue:
           Jane Anne Maclay, m. John S. Tittle of Johnstown, Pa.,
          Emma S. Maclay, m. Wm. H. Bynon of Tipton, Mo.,
          Ellen Maclay, m., 1st, George Fritz, and, 2nd, Robert Murphy, others, d. y.,
      others, d. y. (see Egle's *Pennsylvania Genealogies*),
    Rebecca Findlay, m. (2nd w. of) Thomas Sloo, whose 1st w. was Harriet Irwin (see Irwin family),
    Ellenor Findlay, m. Matthew Smith,
    Mary B. Findlay, m. George P. Torrence, Judge,
      Issue:
        Nancy B. Torrence,

James Findlay Torrence,
Joseph Torrence,
John Findlay Torrence, Mayor of Cincinnati,
Mary P. Torrence, m. W. H. Harrison,
Eliza Jane Torrence, m. —— Handy,
Samuel Torrence,
Aaron Torrence, d. August 12, 1893,
William I. Torrence,
Harriet R. Torrence, m. Hugh Stewart,
three others, dec'd,

John Findlay, m. Nov. 24, 1824, Sarah, dau. of Robert Smith, see Irwin family for their issue,

Samuel B. Findlay, m. Elizabeth Duncan, *née* Patterson,

Eliza R. Findlay, d. unm.

JOHN BROWNSON, see preceding page, Major, m. his second cousin, Sarah, dau. of William Smith by his w. Margaret, dau. of William Piper by his w. Sarah McDowell.

Issue:

Margaret Brownson, d. s. p., m. John McDowell,

James Irwin Brownson (Rev.), D.D., LL.D., Pastor of Presbyterian Church of Greensburg, Pa., 1841-9, and for past forty-four years of First Presbyterian Church of Washington, Pa., President of Washington College, 1852-53, and of Washington and Jefferson, 1869-70, m., 1st, Mch. 14, 1843, Sarah Ellen Maclay, and, 2nd, Jany. 9, 1855, Eleanor McCullough Acheson,

Issue by 1st wife:

Sarah Smith Brownson, m. Henry R. Whitehill, lawyer, of Deer Lodge, Montana,

Issue:

Margaret Brownson Whitehill, d. y.,
James Brownson Whitehill,

John Maclay Brownson, m. Mary Conrad, dec'd,

Issue:

Merle Conrad Brownson,
James Maclay Brownson, d. y.,

Elliott C. Brownson, d. s. p.,
Ellen Maclay Brownson,
Mary R. Brownson, d. unm.,

Issue by 2nd wife:

James Irwin Brownson, lawyer,
Mary W. Brownson,
Marcus A. Brownson (Rev.), D.D., pastor of First Presbyterian Church of Detroit, m. Julia Janvier Bush, dec'd,

Issue:

George Bush Brownson, d. y.,

Margaret McK. Brownson, m. Edwin Linton, professor in Washington and Jefferson College,

Issue:

Eleanor Brownson Linton,
Edwin Linton,

Robert M. Brownson,
Alexander Acheson Brownson,
Lauretta Morgan Brownson,
Robert S. Brownson, M.D., Major 136th Pennsylvania Vols., d. s. p.,
m. Mary, daughter of Alexander Coyle,
eight other children, d. y.

WILLIAM McDOWELL, b. about 1720, son of William McDowell the emigrant, d. Sep. 17, 1812, aged ninety-two, m. Mary Maxwell, who d. Apr. 9, 1808, aged seventy-seven.
Issue:
    WILLIAM McDOWELL, Captain, probably the one in the Revolutionary War, d. June 19, 1835, aged eighty-five.
    JOHN McDOWELL, LL.D., studied for the ministry, but, owing to illness which affected his voice, turned to the profession of law, was Provost of the University of Pennsylvania, and some time President of St. John's College, Annapolis, d. near Mercersburg, Pa., Dec. 22, 1820, aged sixty-nine,
    SUSAN McDOWELL, d. May 17, 1839, aged eighty-six, m. John Martin,
    child, d. y.,
    NATHAN McDOWELL, d. Feb. 1, 1830, aged seventy-one,
    ALEXANDER McDOWELL, d. Feb. 9, 1816, aged fifty-six,
    MARY McDOWELL, d. May 9, 1799, m. Dr. Magaw,
    ANDREW McDOWELL, M.D., d. Jany. 13, 1846, aged eighty-three,
    MARGARET McDOWELL, d. Feb. 17, 1853, aged eighty-seven, m. Mathias Maris,
    NANCY McDOWELL, d. June 6, 1848, aged eighty,
    PATRICK McDOWELL, d. Apr. 24, 1846, aged seventy-six,
    THOMAS McDOWELL, d. Apr. 4, 1851, aged seventy-eight, m. Mary C. Davidson, dec'd,
    Issue:
        MARY M. McDOWELL, dec'd, m. Rev. A. K. Nelson, dec'd,
        Issue:
            Thomas McDowell Nelson, of Chambersburg, bridge builder,
        CATHARINE McDOWELL, m. Rev. N. G. White of New Haven, Pa.,
        Issue:
            Anna M. White, m. —— Neff,
            Henry White, M.D., practising medicine at Connellsville, Pa.,
        WILLIAM HENRY McDOWELL, of Chambersburg, m. Jane C. McFarland, who d. Mch., 1893,
        Issue:

Mary McDowell, d. y.,
Lizzie P. McDowell, d. unm., August, 1892,
Thomas H. McDowell, of Leavenworth, Kan., unm.,
John M. McDowell, of Chambersburg, lawyer, m.
Clara E. Clendenin,
Issue:
Jane McDowell,
John C. McDowell,
Millon G. McDowell,
Henry C. McDowell, of St. Paul, Minn., unm.,
Annie C. McDowell, unm.,
Willie McDowell, d. y.,
Frank McDowell, d. y.,
Edward McDowell, d. y.,
HUGH D. McDOWELL, d. s. p.,
JOHN ALEXANDER McDOWELL, d. s. p.,
SUSAN AGNES McDOWELL, d. s. p.

SARAH McDOWELL, dau. of William McDowell the emigrant, m. William Piper, who was a Captain against French and Indians, and, for his services in Bouquet's expedition, received a grant of land on Warrior's Run, in what is now Northumberland County, on which he afterwards resided.
Issue:
MARGARET PIPER, b. Apr. 3, 1765, d. Mercersburg, Feb. 20, 1852, m., 1st, William Smith, who laid out the town of Mercersburg, brother of Robert Smith who m. Elizabeth Irwin (p. 62), and s. of William Smith by his w. Mary Smith, and, 2nd, Dec. 5, 1787, her first cousin James Irwin, s. of Archibald Irwin by his w. Jean McDowell,
Issue by 1st husband:
SARAH SMITH, m. her cousin John Brownson, see p. 69,
Issue by 2nd husband,—see Irwin family.

RAMSEY.

THE Rev. William Speer, D.D., now of Washington, Pa., who has long been interested in the family history, and has assisted me greatly in the collection of data as to the descendants, has ascertained that the first James Ramsey in the Chart was born in 1725, and came to America from Glasgow, Scotland. Search has been made, at my order, by Rev. Walter MacLeod, 112 Thirlestane Road, Edinburgh, in the registers covering Glasgow, viz.: City Parish, Barony Parish, and Govan Parish, and no baptism of any James Ramsey, or Ramsay, in 1725 or the year following has been found. Although it is more likely that the emigrant was born elsewhere, and in the year alleged, and merely dwelt in Glasgow before coming to America, nevertheless the following entry in the register of the City Parish may refer to him: "1722 September 20 George Ramsay and Isabel Littlejohn, a lawful son James: witnesses, Robert Littlejohn, Alexander Ramsay." The same couple had a son George, baptized Jany. 23, 1724.

The family tradition makes the emigrant a sea captain by profession, leading us to suppose that he landed at Philadelphia in that capacity. He abandoned the sea at a remarkably early age. His will, dated April 23, 1755, when he was only thirty, or—if the aforesaid baptismal entry refers to him—thirty-three, styles him of "York County, Pa., yeoman." It leaves one-third of his property to his wife Mary, and the residue to his children James Ramsey and Mary Ramsey and any others to be born, his silver watch, shoe buckles and knee buckles, and stock buckle to his son James, and the sleeve buttons to his daughter Mary; the wife to be executrix, with the assistance, if necessary, of William Waugh. The will was probated May 28, 1757, and letters were granted to the widow. He died April 16, 1757.

The statement having been made that he married Mary Porter on Oct. 2, 1746, and that this was after he came to America, it seemed worth while to inquire whether the marriage, which does not appear in the published records of the Philadelphia churches, had taken place in Glasgow. Accordingly the records from August to November, 1746, of the three parishes above named, which remained the only ones of the Kirk of Scotland covering Glasgow, were examined by Rev. Mr. MacLeod, and the tradition is confirmed so far, at least, that the marriage is not mentioned therein. Moreover, between 1725 and 1730 no Mary Porter appears to have been born within those jurisdictions. Porter being a common name, the following couples having children baptized about this time were found (the Scotch records mentioning the wife by her maiden name), viz.,—James Porter and Janet Wilkie, James Porter and Jean Biggar, James Porter and Janet Duncan, John Porter and Margaret Alexander, and James Porter and Elizabeth Lyel. Whether Mary who married Captain James Ramsey was any relation of the Porter family to which Elizabeth who married her son belonged, I do not know. That marriage occurring within twenty years after Captain Ramsey's death, his widow, as to whom I have no trace, may readily have been living.

Issue:
  child, d. y.,
  child, d. y.,
  JAMES RAMSEY, b. June 8, 1751, m. Elizabeth Porter, see below,
  MARY RAMSEY, b. July 17, 1753 (if the date was 1755, then this was a second Mary, the first dying after Apr. 23, 1755, and then there was only one child older than James, there having been only four children in all), d. July 16, 1825, m. James Agnew, of the same family as D. Hayes Agnew, M.D., and Rev. B. L. Agnew, D.D., of Philadelphia.

JAMES RAMSEY, b. June 8, 1751, above named, was known as Major Ramsey, but I cannot find that he served during the Revolutionary War. He is said, in McBride's *Pioneer Biography*, to have been an elder of Rev. Matthew Lind's Associate Church at Greencastle. Ramsey built a stone mill on the road between Mercersburg and Greencastle, Pa., since known as Heister's Mill, and established a store, but lost heavily by the spoiling of a cargo of flour at sea on its way to England. He bought at Sheriff's sale, Sep. 2, 1794, the site of Ligonier, Westmoreland Co., and removed to a house about half a mile from the present town. He died of apoplexy. He m. Feb. 15, 1776, Elizabeth Porter, who m., 2ndly, in 1821, Charles Campbell, General, whose son had previously married her daughter. Elizabeth is said to have been daughter of William Porter, and her mother to have been a Percival.

Issue:
  SARAH RAMSEY, b. Jany. 5, 1777, m. Rev. Wm. Speer, see p. 74,
  JOHN RAMSEY, b. Jany. 19, 1779, m. Jane Van Lear, see p. 77,
  MARY RAMSEY, b. Mch. 30, 1781, m. Archibald Irwin, see account of the Irwin family,
  ALICE RAMSEY, b. May 6, 1783, m. William Johnston, see p. 78,
  ELIZABETH RAMSEY, b. Feb. 20, 1785, m. Michael Campbell, see p. 79,
  NANCY RAMSEY, b. Nov. 6, 1787, m. John Sutherland, see p. 81,
  NELLIE RAMSEY (?), if there was such a child, she d. inf.,
  JAMES PORTER RAMSEY, b. Aug. 17, 1794, merchant in Chillicothe, Ohio, afterwards removed to Philadelphia, was an elder of First

Associate Reformed Church, resided in Vine Street below Eleventh, where he d. July 6, 1834, bu. Old Scots Church, Spruce above Third, m., 1st, Miss McLandburg of Chillicothe, by whom he appears to have had no children, at least none survived him, and he m., 2nd, Jane O., dau. of Rev. John Young, Pastor of Associate Reformed Church at Greencastle, Pa., by his w. Mary, dau. of George Clarke,
> Issue by 2nd wife:
> MARY ELIZABETH RAMSEY, d. at Danville, Ky., about 1836, aged about four years.

SARAH RAMSEY, b. Jany. 5, 1777, eldest child of Maj. Ramsey, was killed by lightning near Greensburg, Aug. 8, 1804, m. Nov. 4, 1795, Rev. William Speer, who was b. near Gettysburg, Pa., Sep. 15, 1764, Pastor of Presbyterian Church at Chambersburg, and, from 1802, of the Churches at Unity (near Ligonier) and Greensburg, d. Apr. 26, 1829. His sister Elizabeth was the mother of James Buchanan, President of the United States.
> Issue:
> JAMES RAMSEY SPEER, b. Nov. 19, 1796, m. Hettie Morrow, see below,
> MARIA SPEER, b. Aug. 19, 1800, m. Rev. A. O. Patterson, see p. 76,
> ELIZABETH SPEER, b. June 2, 1802, m. John Riddell, see p. 76.

JAMES RAMSEY SPEER, b. Nov. 19, 1796, above named, grad. M.D., practised medicine in Pittsburgh from the year 1825, d. Sep. 6, 1891, in his ninety-fifth year, m. July 19, 1821, Hettie, dau. of Paul Morrow. She was b. Jany. 10, 1802, d. June 30, 1887.
> Issue:
> William Speer (Rev.), D.D., for several years missionary in China, Secretary of Presbyterian Board of Education in Philadelphia, now residing in Washington, Pa., m., 1st, Cornelia, dau. of Alexander Brackenridge, she d. Macao, China, in 1847, her only issue dying also, and he married, 2nd, Elizabeth Blaine Ewing, dau. of John H. Ewing, Member of Congress, her mother being aunt of James G. Blaine, Secy. of State, etc.,
>> Issue by 2nd wife:
>> John Ewing Speer, A.M. (Princeton), lawyer, residing in McKeesport, m. his cousin Cornelia B. Kuhn,
>>> Issue:
>>> Elizabeth Breading Speer,
>> Henrietta Morrow Speer,
>> Breading Speer, m. Frances Emma, dau. of James B. Wilson,
>>> Issue:
>>> James Wilson Speer,
>> three, d. y.,
> Mary J. Spear, m. John S. Kuhn, M.D., who d. 1883,

Issue:
  Alice Kuhn, m. John McIntyre,
    Issue:
      John Kuhn McIntyre,
      Mary Kuhn McIntyre,
      Cornelia B. McIntyre,
      Katherine McIntyre,
      two, d. inf.,
  Hettie Morrow Kuhn, m. Edward L. Dunbar,
    Issue:
      William K. Dunbar,
      Fannie Ramsey Dunbar,
      Sarah Ramsey Dunbar,
  Cornelia B. Kuhn, m. John Ewing Speer, above,
  Fannie Ramsey Kuhn, d. 1887, m. James H. Scott,
    Issue:
      John Kuhn Scott,
      Mary Ella Scott,
      Gertrude Scott,
  James Spear Kuhn, m. Ella, dau. of James O'Neil of McKeesport, no issue,
  William Speer Kuhn, m. Katherine, dau. of Jerome Hill of St. Louis,
    Issue:
      Wendell Speer Kuhn,

James Postlethwaite Speer, Major 11th Regt. Penna. Reserves, m. Annie R. Blair, dau. of Gen. William Robinson,

Lydia Morrow Speer, d. 1878, m. Francis D. Rigdon, d. 1870,
  Issue:
    Hettie Morrow Rigdon, m. Mark C. Berry,
      Issue:
        Maxwell Berry,
        Rigdon Berry,
        Margaret Berry,
        inf., d. y.,
    Rebe Rigdon, d. y.,
    Laura Rigdon, d. y.,

Alexander Morrow Speer, b. Oct. 28, 1830, M.D., of Pittsburgh, Surgeon 12th Penna. Inf. in Civil War, m. 1872 Ellen Caroline, b. Aug., 1838, dau. of John Bissell of Pittsburgh by his w. Nancy Semple,
  Issue:
    John Bissell Speer, b. Jany. 23, 1873,
    Alexander Morrow Speer, b. Oct. 19, 1876,

Sarah Ramsey Speer, unm.,

Charles Edward Speer, Vice-Pres. First Nat. Bank of Pittsburgh, m. June 13, 1861, Sarah Kennedy Dawson, dau. of John Littleton Dawson by his w. Mary Clarke,
  Issue:
    Mary Clarke Speer, unm.,
    Ettie Morrow Speer, m. Charles A. Painter,
      Issue:
        Mary Lothrop Painter,
        Charles Albert Painter,

John Littleton Dawson Speer, m. Margaret L. Taylor,
Issue:
Charles Edward Speer,
Louise Dawson Speer, unm.,
Charles Edward Speer, unm.,
John Zantzinger Speer, m. Kate, dau. of Joseph McKnight,
Issue:
Margaret Acheson Speer,
James Ramsey Speer,
Joseph McKnight Speer,
Henrietta Zantzinger Speer,
Nellie McKnight Speer,
two children, d. inf.

MARIA SPEER, b. Aug. 19, 1800, dau. of Rev. William and Sarah Speer, p. 74, d. Oct. 26, 1889, m. Nov. 11, 1823, Rev. Andrew Oliphant Patterson, D.D., b. Aug. 1, 1796, Pastor of Presbyterian Church at Mt. Pleasant, Westmoreland Co., Pa., afterwards at Beaver, Pa., and afterwards at New Lisbon, Ohio, d. Dec. 14, 1868.
Issue:
William Speer Patterson, M.D., d. unm. in California in 1856,
Sarah Anna Patterson, m. John S. Earhart, Capt.,
Issue:
Maria S. Earhart, unm.,
John Ewing Patterson, M.D., d. s. p. Oct. 16, 1890, m. Ella C. Bell, widow,
James Ramsey Patterson, unm.,
Alice Caroline Patterson, of Glendale, Ohio, unm.,
Virginia Oliphant Patterson, m. George S. Bishop of Glendale, O.,
Issue:
Maria Speer Bishop, unm.

ELIZABETH SPEER, b. June 2, 1802, dau. of Rev. William and Sarah Speer, p. 74, d. Apr. 4, 1856, m. John Riddell, grad. A.M. at Jefferson College, practised law in Erie, Pa., d. 1837, s. of Rev. John Riddell, D.D., Pastor of Associate Reformed Church at Robinson Run, Pa.
Issue:
John William Riddell, lawyer in Erie and afterwards in Pittsburgh, now of California, m. Margaret, dec'd,
Issue:
Margaret Riddell, m. Joseph Wainwright of Pittsburgh,
Issue:
Josephine Wainwright,
John Riddell Wainwright,
Speer Riddell, banker, d. unm. San Francisco, Oct. 23, 1884, aged fifty-six,
James Riddell, druggist, d. unm. Glen Riddell, Santa Clara Co., Cal., July 3, 1888, aged fifty-four,

DeWitt Clinton Riddell, of Santa Cruz, Cal., m. Philinda, dau. of
J. J. Dorland of Gilroy, Cal.,
> Issue:
>> Philinda L. Riddell, unm.,
>> DeWitt Speer Riddell, unm.,
>> Sarah Elizabeth Riddell, d. aged 1 y.,

Harriet Elizabeth Riddell, m. Samuel G. Magill,
> Issue:
>> Elizabeth E. Magill, d. unm.,
>> Thomas Whitehead Magill, of Chicago, m. Jennie M. Ware, no issue,
>> Henry E. Magill, m. Lulu Richardson,
>>> Issue:
>>>> Elizabeth Magill,
>>>> William R. Magill,
>> Helen Davenport Magill, m. Frederic Earll Briggs,
>>> Issue:
>>>> Earll Briggs,
>>>> Helen D. Briggs,
>>>> Stanley Briggs,
>>>> Alice Briggs,
>> John Riddell Magill, unm.,
>> Samuel G. Magill, unm.,
>> Harriet Elizabeth Magill, unm.

JOHN RAMSEY, b. Jany. 19, 1779, son of Maj. James Ramsey, p. 73, laid out the town of Ligonier, and was Colonel, and, having been proprietor of the inn at Mercersburg, removed to Pittsburgh, and had the hotel at which dinner and ball were given to Lafayette in 1825. He removed from Pittsburgh about 1831, and died of cholera at Maysville, Ky., in 1833. He m. Nov. 4, 1802, Jane Van Lear, d. Mch. 26, 1828, dau. of Matthew Van Lear by his wife Mary Irwin (see account of that family).
> Issue:
>> JAMES RAMSEY, b. Aug. 29, 1803, d. July 25, 1835, m. Oct. 22, 1832, Eliza Caldwell,
>>> Issue:
>>>> Jane Olivia Ramsey, d. May 3, 1892, m. Oct. 17, 1861, James H. Buckner, M.D., of Cincinnati,
>>>>> Issue:
>>>>>> William Taliaferro Buckner, b. Apr. 19, 1863, m. Oct. 3, 1893, Elizabeth I., dau. of Carter B. Harrison, see Chart,
>>>>>> Harry Alexander Buckner, b. Aug. 24, 1866,
>> MATHEW RAMSEY, b. June 1, 1805, d. unm. July 20, 1826,
>> JOHN RAMSEY, b. Dec. 31, 1807, d. unm. Mch. 4, 1834,
>> MARY JANE RAMSEY, b. Dec. 4, 1809, d. unm. Sep. 21, 1830,
>> ELIZA ANN RAMSEY, b. Jany. 2, 1812, resided at the White House during Pres. William Henry Harrison's administration, d. unm. May 26, 1845,
>> SARAH LOUISA RAMSEY, b. Feb. 28, 1814, dec'd, m. July 31, 1838, (2nd w. of) William Irwin of Cincinnati, cousin of her mother,

Issue, see account of Irwin family,

SOPHIA ALICE RAMSEY, b. Nov. 27, 1816, d. unm. Jany. 19, 1835,
NANCY CAROLINE RAMSEY, b. Aug. 28, 1819, d. unm. May 2, 1836,
SUSAN EMMA RAMSEY, b. May 27, 1821, d. unm. Jany. 4, 1846,
ELLEN RAMSEY, b. Feb. 4, 1823, d. y. Aug. 16, 1823,
FRANCES HARRIET RAMSEY, b. July 8, 1824, d. unm. June 7, 1844—these children were celebrated for personal beauty.

ALICE RAMSEY, b. May 6, 1783, dau. of Maj. James Ramsey, p. 73, d. Apr. 12, 1851, m. at Mercersburg, Pa., Sep. 15, 1801, William Johnston, b. June 7, 1776, salt manufacturer near Saltsburg, Pa., son of John Johnston soldier of the Revolution, Captain, by his 1st wife Rebecca Smith.
Issue:
  REBECCA SMITH JOHNSTON, b. July 2, 1802, dec'd, m. John Miller of Gettysburg, civil engineer, killed in a mob in Baltimore in 1840,
  Issue:
    William Johnston Miller, served in Mexican War, dec'd, m.
    —— Spicer,
      Issue:
      seven children,
    James Henry Miller, served in Mexican and Civil Wars, dec'd, m. ——,
      Issue:
      twelve children,
    Robert Miller, served in Civil War, unm.,
    John Thomas Miller, served in Civil War, d. s. p.,
    Allie Miller, m., 1st, Dr. Burnum of Baltimore, and, 2nd, Col. Hewitt of St. Paul,
    Mary Elizabeth Miller, d. s. p., m. Capt. H. Schreiner of Washington, D.C.,
    Rebecca Emma Miller, of Washington, D.C., unm.,
  JAMES RAMSEY JOHNSTON, b. Oct. 29, 1803, dec'd, m. Eliza M., dau. of Rev. Francis Laird, D.D., of Westmoreland Co., Pa.,
  Issue:
    Francis Laird Johnston, d. unm.,
    William Johnston, dec'd, m. ——,
  JOHN JOHNSTON, b. Aug. 20, 1807, d. inf.,
  ROBERT SMITH JOHNSTON, b. Aug. 21, 1809, Colonel in militia, d. June 23, 1846, m. Jane, dau. of Rev. David Kirkpatrick, D.D., of Westmoreland Co., Pa.,
  Issue:
    Amey Eliza Johnston, d. inf.,
    Mary Elizabeth S. Johnston, m. Rev. Samuel Earp,

Issue:
>Jobn Kirkpatrick Earp,
>Mary Baldy Earp, d. y.,
>Cornelia Fuller Earp,
>William Henry Hinsdale Earp,

WILLIAM POSTLETHWAITE (or POSTELWAGTH) JOHNSTON, b. Nov. 12, 1815, fought for Texan independence, killed in the massacre of Goliad, d. unm.,

ELIZABETH RAMSEY JOHNSTON, b. Sep. 3, 1818, now of Linneus, Mo., m. Feb. 27, 1844, Thomas W. Robinson of Saltsburg, Indiana Co., Pa., who was b. Feb. 24, 1814, d. in Missouri Feb. 4, 1882,

>Issue:
>Robert Edgar Robinson, b. Dec. 27, 1844, d. Sep. 15, 1845,
>William Johnston Robinson, b. Mch. 9, 1846, d. Dec. 14, 1891, m. 1885 Agnes Fulton of Glasgow, Scotland,
>>Issue:
>>Robert Johnston Robinson,
>>Grace May Robinson,
>Alice Ramsey Robinson, b. Oct. 11, 1847, d. Feb. 26, 1878, m. Apr. 25, 1873, F. N. Robertson,
>>Issue:
>>Grace Robertson, b. June 17, 1874,
>>Bessie Robertson, d. y.,
>>Alice Robertson, d. y.,
>Robert Johnston Robinson, b. Sep. 29, 1849, of Linneus, Mo., unm.,
>David Robinson, b. Aug. 9, 1852, d. July 3, 1853.

ELIZABETH RAMSEY, b. Feb. 20, 1785, dau. of Maj. James Ramsey, p. 73, resided near Blairsville, Pa., d. Sep. 1, 1858, m. Oct. 7, 1806, Michael Campbell, b. 1781, d. 1833, son of Gen. Charles Campbell.

Issue:

CHARLES BUTLER CAMPBELL, b. Aug. 25, 1807, d. unm. Aug. 30, 1863,

JAMES RAMSEY CAMPBELL, b. Jany. 17, 1809, d. unm. Oct. 2, 1880,

ELIZABETH RAMSEY CAMPBELL, b. Jany. 26, 1811, d. June 5, 1872, m. Dec. 12, 1832, Absalom Woodward, killed by Indians while in charge of U. S. mail between Salt Lake and California in 1850,

>Issue:
>Elizabeth Porter Woodward, d. y.,
>Isabella Woodward, of Indiana, Pa., unm.,
>Mary Lavinia Woodward, m. Daniel Smith,
>>Issue:
>>Elizabeth Campbell-Smith, d. unm.,

Absalom Woodward Smith,
Ruth Smith,
Isabella Rebecca Smith,
Simon Woodward, d. y.,
Michael Campbell Woodward, m. Olive Prothero, no issue,
Margaret Porter Woodward,

MICHAEL CAMPBELL, b. Feb. 20, 1813, d. s. p. Xenia, Ohio, 1836,

MARGARET CLARK CAMPBELL, b. Apr. 12, 1815, d. s. p. July 25, 1891, m. Oct. 21, 1835, Nathaniel Porter Turner,

THOMAS CAMPBELL, b. Mch. 8, 1819, d. Villisca, Iowa, June 6, 1887, m. Eliza J. Wilson, d. Sep. 10, 1889,

Issue:

  James W. Campbell, m. Aug. 10, 1868, Ida J. Hoyt,

  Issue:
    Frank H. Campbell,
    Thomas M. Campbell,
    Anna Campbell, d. y.,
    Clark Vern Campbell,
    Myrtle Campbell,

  Elizabeth Ramsey Campbell, dec'd, m. Samuel Jack of Farmington, Ill.,

  Issue:
    Lyda Jack,
    Porter Jack,
    Maud Jack,
    Lizzie Jack,

  J. Milton Campbell, of Yorktown, Iowa, m., 1st, Jany. 13, 1876, Maggie M. Dunbar, who d. Mch. 27, 1887, and, 2nd, Nov. 1, 1888, Mary E. McClelland,

  Issue by 1st wife:
    Bertha Edith Campbell,
    Lester Campbell,
    Lyle Campbell, d. inf.,
    Ethel Grace Campbell,
    Ruthetta Campbell, d. inf.,
  Issue by 2nd wife:
    Earle Scott Campbell,
    Russell Harrison Campbell,

  Thomas Scott Campbell, d. Mch. 27, 1889, m. Nov. 11, 1885, Alice M., daughter of John Work of Bardolph, Ill.,

  Issue:
    Walter Scott Campbell,
    Lester Work Campbell,

  Wilson Marshall Campbell, m. June 6, 1882, Alice M., dau. of James Park of Bardolph, Ill., no issue,

SARAH JANE CAMPBELL, b. June 17, 1821, d. June, 1853, m. Thomas Wilson,

Issue:
    Anna Eliza Wilson, d. unm.,
    Joseph Campbell Wilson,
MARY ALICE CAMPBELL, b. Jany. 14, 1823, dec'd, m. June 17, 1846, Archibald Coleman,
    Issue:
        Michael Campbell Coleman, d. y.,
        Archibald McClelland Coleman, of Blairsville, m. Emma Jane, dau. of Joseph G. Turner, no issue,
        Sarah Alice Coleman, d. 1887, m. Arthur De Voe, M.D.,
            Issue:
                Mary Grace De Voe,
                Archibald Coleman De Voe,
                Ralph Godwin De Voe,
        Charles Butler Campbell Coleman, of Blairsville, m. Isabel Cummins,
            Issue:
                Margaretta Alice Coleman,
        Margaret Elizabeth Coleman, d. y.,
JOHN RAMSEY CAMPBELL, b. Oct. 26, 1826, d. Jany. 2, 1884, m. April 11, 1853, Agnes Jane Hill,
    Issue:
        James Campbell, m. Laura Warner,
            Issue:
                Agnes Jane Campbell,
                Mary M. Campbell,
                John Ramsey Campbell,
        Elizabeth R. Campbell, d. y.,
GEORGE WASHINGTON CAMPBELL, b. Sep. 1, 1828, of Peabody, Kansas, m. Sarah E., dau. of William Giberson of Sunbury, Pa.,
    Issue:
        William Giberson Campbell,
        Elizabeth Ramsey Campbell, m. T. M. Huffman, M.D.,
            Issue:
                Kathryn Huffman.

NANCY RAMSEY, b. Nov. 6, 1787, dau. of Maj. James Ramsey, p. 73, d. Hamilton, Ohio, March 21, 1855, m. May, 1810, (3rd wife of) John Sutherland, b. Caithness, Scotland, in 1770, Commissary under Gen. Meigs in War of 1812, d. Hamilton, Ohio, in 1834, see McBride's *Pioneer Biography.*
    Issue:
        ELIZABETH ST.CLAIR SUTHERLAND, b. 1811, d. unm. about 1852,
        MARY ANNE SUTHERLAND, b. 1814, d. at North Bend May 28, 1893, m. June 16, 1836, Carter Bassett Harrison, d. 1839, son of Pres. William Henry Harrison,

Issue:
    Anna Carter Harrison, m. David W. McClung, Brevet Major U. S. Vols., Collector of U. S. Internal Revenue, resides at North Bend,

SARAH ALICE SUTHERLAND, b. 1817, m. Feb. 21, 1840, Nathaniel Reeder,
  Issue:
    Nathaniel Sutherland Reeder, b. Mch. 3, 1841, of Cincinnati, m. Julia Potter,
      Issue:
        Russell Potter Reeder, b. May 9, 1872,
        Nathaniel Sutherland Reeder, b. May 16, 1875,
    John Sutherland Reeder, b. Nov., 1843,
    Elizabeth Yeatman Reeder, d. y.,
    James Ramsey Reeder, b. Dec., 1852,
    Carter Harrison Reeder, d. y.,

JOHN FINDLAY SUTHERLAND, b. 1819, unm.,
JANE RAMSEY SUTHERLAND, b. 1822, unm.,
ISABELLA SUTHERLAND, b. 1825, m. Oct. 6, 1864, Dr. Joseph S. McNeeley, Surgeon U. S. Navy, now dec'd,
  Issue:
    Joseph Sutherland McNeeley, m. Feb. 4, 1891, Mary H. Taylor,
NANCY RAMSEY SUTHERLAND, b. 1828, d. unm. 1885.

SYMMES.

MATHER'S *Magnalia Christi Americana* contains a sketch of Rev. Zechariah Symmes, the emigrant, giving the name of his father and grandfather. It quotes from a record made by Rev. William Symmes in, to use Mather's words, "a book which was made by a godly preacher that was hid"—*Quere*, the book or the preacher?—in the house of Rev. Zechariah's grandfather during the Marian persecution. The record closes thus: "Both my father and mother were favourers of the Gospel, and hated idolatry under Queen Mary's persecution. I came by this book by this means: going to Sandwich in Kent to preach the first or second year after I was ordained minister Anno 1587 or 1588, and preaching in Saint Mary's, where Mr. Pawson, an ancient godly preacher, was minister, who knew my parents well, and me too at school, he after I had finished my sermons, came and brought me this book for a present, acquainting me with the above mentioned circumstances. I charge my sons Zechariah and William . . . that you never defile yourselves with any idolatry or superstition . . . Scripsi Dec. 6, 1602." It thus appears that the parents of Rev. William were married before November, 1558, when the reign of "Bloody Mary" closed with her death; that Rev. William, to have been of canonical age for ordination to the priesthood in the Church of England, and we are not to presume a dispensation, was born before 1562; and that to have been known while at school to Rev. Thomas Pawson, who became Rector of St. Mary's during Rev. William's youth, he probably attended the grammar school at Sandwich founded in 1564 by Sir Roger Manwood. From this I have inferred that the family belonged to that neighbourhood. The only marriage of any of the name, in its varied spelling, appearing prior to 1550 in the registers of St. Mary's and St. Peter's parishes, Sandwich, the former searched from 1538, and the latter from 1549, was: "1551 Will'm. Si'me and Elizabeth Iden the 13 of Ap'll." If this was the grandfather of Rev. Zechariah, there is nothing to show that Elizabeth was his only wife before Queen Mary's death; for another could have been married in some neighbouring parish, whither William seems to have removed. The only baptism in either of the three parishes into which Sandwich is divided, of any person of this surname, down to 1570, St. Clement's register, however, beginning in 1563, was: "1553 John Sym sonn of William Sym 25 Oct." There are many Symmes, Symes, Symme, Syme, etc. wills in the archidiaconal court at Canterbury, but they will not make a connected pedigree. The will of William Sy'me of Ash next Sandwich, dated Oct.

10, 1573, mentions children William, Richard, and Elizabeth, and wife Sybell, as well as "brothers Robart Sy'me and Mr. Bronnemayde of Canterbury" and kinsman John Neame. The register of Ash, beginning in 1558, contains no entry relating to the name down to 1567, but has been mutilated so that the part covering the last five months of 1561 and first six months of 1562 is missing.

Edward Johnson's *Wonder-Working Providence*, written in 1652, speaks of Rev. Zechariah's and his father's or his wife's father's (*i.e.* his children's grandfather's) sufferings "for Christ's Kingdom," and gives the lines:

> "Come Zachary thou must reedify
> *   *   *   *
> Thy father's spirit doubled is upon
> Thee, Symmes, then war: thy father fighting died.
> In prayer then prove thou a like champion!"

It is not unlikely that Zechariah's brother William was the William Symmes appointed preacher at Leicester in the days of the Commonwealth: for Zechariah's will, dated Jany. 20, 1664-5, shows that "my dear brother Mr. William Symmes" was still living, and the prefix "Mr." in that Century most frequently indicated a minister.

The epitaph of Rev. Zechariah Symmes says that he had lived 49 years and 7 mos. with his virtuous consort, by whom he had thirteen children, five sons and eight daughters. I have no clue as to her maiden name.

The 2nd wife of William, son of Rev. Zechariah, I am inclined to identify with Mary, b. Mch. 8, 1647, daughter of John Carter of Woburn by his wife Elizabeth. When letters of administration were granted on William's estate to his widow, her sureties were Matthew Johnson Senr. and John Carter, both of Woburn. When the inventory was filed, James Convers Senr., Matthew Johnson Senr., and James Convers 2nd were the appraisers. Savage's *Genealogical Dictionary of New England* does not state whom Mary, daughter of John Carter the elder, married: the other children who lived to grow up were Abigail, b. Apr. 24, 1648, Hannah, b. Jany. 19, 1651, and John, b. Feb. 6, 1653, who, or else his father, was the surety aforesaid, while Hannah m. Jany. 1, 1668, James Convers 2nd, one of the appraisers. John Carter 2nd lived until April, 1727, and he and his wife may have been the uncle and aunt mentioned in a letter of Timothy Symmes to his brother William at Weymouth dated June 28, 1707 (see Vinton's *Symmes Memorial*). The bequest in 1681 by Sarah Bowles's will to William Symmes can be explained by supposing his first wife to have been a daughter of said Sarah by her first husband, John Sibley of Charlestown.

TUTHILL.

Browning's *Americans of Royal Descent* gives an ancestral line of the emigrant Tuthill, through Grafton the Chronicler and the Earls of Chester, to Alfred the Great: but I am unable to verify it. It has moreover too many generations of Tuthills in this country. The first Tuthill named in the Chart may have been son of John of Saxlingham, Norfolk, mentioned in the *Visitation of Essex in 1634* as second son of John Tuthill and his w. Elizabeth Woolmer, and grandson of a John Tuthill of Saxlingham. The sons of the elder brother of the first above named John are enumerated, and no Henry appears among them. The records of St. Mary's, Tharston, Norfolk, give the burial of "Elizabeth Tuttell widowe" —could she be John's?—on Feb. 7, 1587, and the burial of Henry Tuthill on Mch. 26, 1618, and the following baptisms of the children of Henry Tuthill (spelling it also Tutthill, Tuttill, and Tuttell) and Alice his wife, viz.: John on Oct. 25, 1607, William on Oct. 29, 1609, Henrye on June 28, 1612, and Elsebeth on Mch. 9, 1616.

William H. Tuthill's *Genealogy* (in chart form) *of the Tuthill and Kent Families* says that the Henry who was born in 1665 married Bethiah Horton in 1706, thus leaving a doubt, which I can not resolve, whether the date is seventeen years too late, or the son Henry, born in 1690, was the child of a former wife. The Rev. Epher Whitaker, D.D., author of *History of Southold*, who has kindly given me much information, believes Bethiah to have been the mother of Henry, and accordingly married in or before 1690. She was born in 1674. The will of her father Jonathan Horton mentions her as wife of Henry Tuthill; but is not dated early enough to settle the point. Jonathan Horton was son of Barnabas, said to have been b. at Mousely, Leicestershire, England, July 13, 1600, emigrated to Hampton, Mass., and afterwards to Southold, and son of a Joseph Horton. Jonathan's wife was Bethiah, daughter of William Wells, Recorder of Southold and Sheriff.

There is a tombstone to "Hanna wife of Henry Tuthill," giving as date of her death "in ye 24th year of her age Dec. 1, 1715." This Henry seems to have been the one born in 1690, his marriage to Phebe Youngs taking place in 1717; so that Hanna was apparently the mother of the Henry who was born in 1715. The later connection of the family with New Jersey strengthens the likelihood of the identity of the Henry born in 1690 with the Henry Tuthill who on Oct. 22, 1711, with Elizabeth Crouch received letters of administration in New Jersey on the estate of Richard

Crouch, or Croutch, of Essex County, New Jersey. It is fair to presume that Henry Tuthill had married Crouch's daughter: thus Hanna, whose tombstone we have mentioned, would have been a Crouch.

The will of the Henry Tuthill who was born in 1715 names his wife Phebe, but whether she was the one who was mother of Mrs. John Cleves Symmes, I do not know. The *Horton Genealogy* says that Phebe, dau. of Caleb Horton, who lived in New Jersey, m. Henry Tuthill. This Phebe was born about 1722. Her descendants are not given in that work. Caleb Horton's will, dated May 16, 1759, and codicil, dated Jany. 2, 1768, mention Phebe, but do not tell us whether she was married or single when they were written.

VARIOUS VIRGINIA FAMILIES.

A CLUE to the ancestry of John Carter, the Virginia Councillor mentioned in the Chart, seemed to be afforded in the will of Edward Carter of Edmonton, Middlesex, esquire, dated and probated in 1682 (*New England Hist. and Geneal. Reg.*, Vol. XLVII.), disposing of much property in Virginia, and speaking of having resided on Nansemond River, showing that he must have been the Col. Edward Carter who was in Virginia about 1660, and who may naturally be supposed to have been brother of John Carter. The will gives to a son Edward " my third part (the whole in three parts to be divided) of and in all those messuages, tenements, lands, and hereditaments in Chalfont St. Peter's, Bucks." It would seem that the last-named property must have been inherited, and the locality the seat of the family. Accordingly, I have had the Carter wills of the archdeaconry of Buckinghamshire examined, but with no result. Probably John Carter's wife Anne, daughter of Cleave Carter, was cousin—in fact, first cousin—of her husband; so there is ground for supposing that the grandmother was a Cleave, particularly as that name was given to one of the seats of the family in Virginia. Otherwise, it would seem strange that the offspring of Sarah Ludlow would perpetuate the family name of another wife. The published lists of London marriage licenses include one Oct. 25, 1611, for John Carter of Stepney, Middlesex, mariner, and Jane Cleaves of All Hallows, Barking, widow of John Cleaves of same, mariner, doubtless relations-in-law, and possibly parents of the Virginia Councillor or of Cleave Carter. Mr. W. G. Stanard finds that John Carter married at least five times, viz.:

1st (at least, as far as known), Jane, dau. of Morgan Glyn, she being buried with her husband and her son George, and, if indeed the first wife, being mother not only of George, but of John Carter, who m. Elizabeth Wormeley, and of Elizabeth, who m. Nathaniel (?) Utie, said Elizabeth Utie being mentioned in her father's will as having received her portion;

2nd, after April, 1655, and before April 9, 1656 (when John Carter speaks of Eltonhead Connaway as his niece), Eleanor, *née* Eltonhead, widow of Capt. William Brocas (see Hayden's *Virginia Genealogies*), this Eleanor being probably the Elenor Carter who is buried with John Carter, and whom Bp. Meade and others have supposed to have been a daughter of Jane, and it is probable that Eleanor had no children by Carter;

3rd, Anne, dau. of Cleave Carter, she being buried with her husband, and appearing to have had no children by Carter, and to have d. in or before 1662, to allow time for Carter to have married again, and have had a son born after Aug. 4, 1663, and before Aug. 4, 1664;

4th, Sarah, dau. of Gabriel Ludlow, she being buried with her husband, and her daughter Sarah, and having died in or before 1668, having been mother not only of Sarah, but also, according to tradition, of Robert, "King Carter," who d. Aug. 4, 1732, in his 69th year;

5th (contract in view of marriage dated Oct. 24, 1668), Elizabeth Sherley of Gloucester County, spinster, she not buried with her husband, but mentioned in his will with her son Charles.

John Carter's will was dated Jany. 3, 1669.

The Thomas and Mary Landon mentioned on the tombstone of Betty, 2nd wife of "King Carter," as her parents, were perhaps the Thomas Landon of Credenhill, gentleman, eldest Groom of His Majesty's Buttery, and Mary called "his now wife" in the will, dated Feb. 6, 1679, of his kinsman, another Thomas Landon, who styles himself "of Monington Stradell, in the parish of Vonchurch in County Hereford, gentleman, yeoman to the Buttery of King Charles I., and now in the same office to King Charles II." Betty was born after the will was made. Credenhill is the birthplace intended on Betty Carter's tombstone. Thomas of Credenhill aforesaid was the son of Silvanus Landon of St. Martin's in the Fields, Middlesex, gent., whose will also was executed prior to Betty's birth. Silvanus's 2nd wife was Frances, *née* Scott, widow of Sir Anthony St. Leger. Thomas, son of Silvanus, had a son Thomas, and it is possible that he took a wife named Mary, lived at Credenhill, and was father of Betty. Among the MSS. of Sir Hans Sloane in the British Museum is a letter addressed to him by a Mary Landon dated Aug. 24, 1716, expressing a design "to spend her days in the service of God and the study of philosophy." From the Credenhill branch of the family descended Letitia Elizabeth Landon, who wrote over the initials L. E. L. After figuring out the children that "King Carter" had by Judith Armistead, the tombstone giving the number of them, I am obliged to contradict the Carter Family Tree, and place Anne wife of Benjamin Harrison among the children by Betty, *née* Landon.

The tradition of any near relationship between the William Churchill of the Chart and the celebrated Duke of Marlborough is contradicted by there having been at North Aston, Oxfordshire, where William's will says he was born, a Henry Churchill who died as early as 1629, distinct from the Duke's ancestral line. This Henry is mentioned in the will of a Thomas Churchill of Blackthorne, Oxfordshire, dated Mch. 29, 1615. Neither of these persons appears in the account of the Churchills of Muston, Dorset, in Burke's *Landed Gentry*, although the emigrant to Virginia used as a seal the arms of that family. The will of Henry of North Aston names three sons,—John, Henry, and Justinian. William the emigrant is erroneously said in the Chart to have died in 1711. He died on Nov. 8, 1710.

The mother of Sarah Ludlow, who m. John Carter, appears to have been

Phillis, the wife who survived Gabriel Ludlow, and who, as far as is known, was his only wife. Her will, leaving everything to said Gabriel's children, each of whom she called "my son" or "my daughter," gives no clue as to her maiden name, and the compiler of the Ludlow pedigree mentioned in the Introduction has failed to ascertain it. Gabriel Ludlow is mentioned as a kinsman in the will of George Willoughby, who was a trader in the East Indies. He was son of Albinus Willoughby whose nuncupative will, made Aug. 1, 1606, named Gabriel Pile as an overseer, which may indicate that the relationship between George Willoughby and Gabriel Ludlow was through the Piles (see the Chart). The uncommonness of the names "Albinus," or "Alban," and "Phillis" tempts us to identify Phillis Ludlow with Phillis Wakelyn, one of the four daughters of Alban Wakelyn of Henley on Thames, Oxfordshire, whose will was dated April 21, 1602, and probated Feb. 10, 1602-3, but I can not trace the family later, except that Mary Wakelyn, who m. Matthew Bentley of Banbury, afterwards m. —— Washington, and as "Mary Bentley *alias* Washington" took letters *d. b. n. c. t. a.* on April 30, 1624. Alban Wakelyn was originally of Eydon, Northamptonshire, and was a grandson of Alban Butler of Aston le Walls, and, although the wife of Alban Wakelyn mentioned in his will was named Amye, he is known to have married—and this former wife may have been Phillis's mother—Anne, daughter of Robert Washington and aunt of Rev. Lawrence Washington, whose son was the emigrant ancestor of George Washington.

In regard to the Bassetts, Mrs. Lewis Washington dissents from my determination of the parentage of the emigrant.

OMISSIONS FROM THE CHART.

THE following, gathered from *L'Art de Vérifier les Dates*, is the descent from Sancho III., King of Navarre, mentioned in the Chart, to Raymond Berenger, Count of Provence, also mentioned in the Chart.

Sancho III., m. 1001 Munie Elvire, dau. of Sancho Garcia and granddau. of Garcia Sanchez, Count of Castille, and had by her, their second son,

Ferdinand I. of Castille and Leon, d. Dec. 27, 1065, for whom Castille was made a separate kingdom by treaty of 1033, pursuant to which he m. Sancha, who d. Nov. 7, 1067, sister of Bermudo III., King of Leon. Ferdinand and Sancha's second son was

Alfonso VI., King of Leon, d. June, 1109, m. Constance, d. 1092, dau. of Robert I., Duke of Burgundy, and had by her an only child,

Urraca, m., 1st, in 1090, Raymond Berenger, Count of Amous and Gallicia, d. 1108, brother of Pope Callixtus II., and son of William, Count of Burgundy, or Franche Comté, whose descent from Charlemagne and Charles Martel is given in the Chart. By Raymond, Urraca had a son

Alfonso Raymond, or Alfonso VIII., King of Castille and Leon, m. 1153 Richilde, and had

Sancha, m. Jany. 18, 1174, Alfonso II., King of Arragon, who d. Apr. 25, 1196, and by whom she had a second son,

Alfonso, Count of Provence, d. 1209, m. 1193 Gersande, by whom he had

Raymond Berenger, Count of Provence.

The following is the descent from Margaret, Queen of Scotland, heiress of the Saxon Kings of England, mentioned in the Chart, to Humphrey de Bohun, Earl of Hereford, Etc., therein mentioned.

Malcolm III. "Caen Mohr" and Margaret had, besides Matilda mentioned in the Chart, other children, and among them a son,

St. David (David I.), King of Scotland, d. May 23, 1153, m. Maud, widow of Simon de S. Liz, and dau. of Waldeof, Earl of Northumberland, and by her had a son,

Henry, Earl of Huntingdon, d. in 1152, m. Ada, sister of William, Earl of Warren and Surrey, mentioned in the Chart, and dau. of William, Earl of Warren and Surrey, by his w. Elizabeth, dau. of the Count of Vermandois, her descent from the French Kings and from Bernard, King of Italy, appearing in the Chart, and by said Ada, Henry had a daughter,

Margaret, who, after death of Conan le Petit, Earl of Richmond, and claimant to Brittany, her 2nd (?) husband, who d. Feb. 20, 1171, m., 3rd, (King John's charter to the canons of Lanthony) Humphrey de Bohun, Earl of Hereford and Constable of England, who by her (*Fundatorum Progenies*, transcribed from chronicles of Lanthony Abbey by Robt. Glover) had

Henry de Bohun, Earl of Hereford, and Constable of England, d. June 1, 1220, m. Matildis, dau. of Geoffrey FitzPiers, Earl of Essex, and by her had

Humphrey de Bohun, Earl of Hereford and Essex, and Constable of England, d. Sep. 24, 1275, m. Matildis, dau. of Count of Eu in Normandy, and by her had

Humphrey de Bohun, d. in 1265, m. Alienor, dau. of Wm. de Breuse, and by her had

Humphrey de Bohun, Earl of Hereford and Essex, and Constable of England, d. 1298, m. Matilda, dau. of William de Fenes, and by her had

Humphrey de Bohun, Earl of Hereford and Essex, and Constable of England, who m. Elizabeth, dau. of King Edward I.

INDEX.

The Arabic numerals refer to the page of the text. The persons in the Chart are indicated by Roman numerals corresponding with the Century of our Lord during which they were either born or died.

Abrahall, 27, 28.
Acheson, 69.
Adams, 62.
Addison, 17.
Agar or Agard, 25.
Agnew, 56, 73.
Alençon, Count of, XIII.
Alexander, 73.
Allen, 19.
Alston, XIX.
Ambler, 36.
Anderson, 21.
Andrews, 7, XV.
Angelus or Angela, XII.-XIII.
Armistead, 13-21, 37, 38, 88, XVII.
Arundel, 9, 10, XIV.
Ashburnham, 25.
Assistance from various persons, 5, 6, 7, 8, 18, 23, 27, 39, 41, 53, 67, 72, 85.
Atkinson, 57, 58.
Atwater, 24.
Ayala, 6, XIII.-XV.
Aylmer, 13.
Ayres, 64.
Bacon, 22-26, 27, XV.-XVII.
Ball, 18.
Baltzell, 63.
Banks, XIX.
Barclay, 51.
Barnum, 78.
Barroso, XIII.-XIV.
Barzizi, 50.
Bassett, 16, 22, 24, 27-33, 36, 39, 40, 89, XVII.-XVIII.
Bay, 55.
Baylor, 18, 36.
Beaumont, 8, XIV.
Beck, 55.
Bedell, 34, XVII.
Belfield, 35.
Bell, 76.

Bentley, 89.
Berkeley, 11, 12, 17, 28, 36, 37.
Bernard, King of Italy, and line of Vermandois, 5, 90, VIII.-XI.
Bernard, XVII.
Berry, 75.
Beverley, 14.
Biggar, 73.
Bishop, 76.
Bissell, 75.
Blaine, 51, 74.
Blair, 47, 75.
Blofield, 35.
Blois, Counts of, XII.
Blount, 6, 7, 12, XIV.-XVI.
Boggs, 53.
Bohun, 90, XIV.
Bonner, XIX.
Booth, 18, 21, 66.
Boulstrode or Bulstrode, 24, XV., XVI.
Bowles, 14, 17, 84.
Boyd, 52.
Brabant, Dukes of, XIII.
Brackenridge, 74.
Bradby, 48.
Braden, 61.
Bradley, 51.
Branen, 56.
Brent, 43.
Breuse, 90.
Brian or Brien, 9, 10, XIV.
Briggs, 77.
Brocas, 87.
Brock, 27.
Brounemayde, 84.
Brown, 52, 60.
Browne, 31, 32, 33.
Brownson, 68-70.
Buchanan, 74.
Buckner, 77.
Buckus, 32.

91

Burgess, 18.
Burgundian Kings, 12, V.
Burnet, 32.
Burroughs, 23.
Burwell, 14, 16–18, 22–23, 34–38, 47, 50, XVI.–XVIII.
Bush, 69.
Butler, 89.
Button, 35.
Butts, 18, 52.
Bynon, 69.
Byrd, 14, 15.
Cabell, 51.
Cage, XV.
Caldwell, 77.
Campbell, 73, 79, XVIII.
Canfield, 59.
Cantelupe, 11.
Capet, Hugh, and his male line in France and Burgundy, 90, X.–XIV.
Cargill, 48.
Carlovingian Kings, etc., see Charles Martel and Bernard and Louis d'Outremer.
Carr, 51.
Carson, 61.
Carter, 5, 14–15, 32, 36, 50, 84, 87–88, XVII.–XVIII.
Cary, 14, 15, 16, 19, 20, 22, 29, 30, 39–40, 48, XV.–XVII.
Castille, Kings of, 5, 90, XII.–XIII.
Chamberlayne, 31.
Champe, 15.
Chapman, 60.
Charles Martel, Pepin le Bref, Charlemagne, and Louis Debonnaire, 4, 5, 90, VIII.–IX.
Chaworth, XIII.
Cheek, XIX.
Chicheley, 13.
Chichester, 28.
Chittenden, XVII.
Churchill, 14–16, 30, 48, 88, XVII.–XVIII.
Claiborne, 31, 33, 52.
Clarke, 74, 75.
Claypoole, 61.
Cleave or Cleaves, 87.
Clendenin, 71.
Cleves, XVIII.
Clovis, and his male descendants in France and Spain, 4, 5, 12, 90, V.–XII.
Cobham, 9, XIV.
Cocke, 52.
Cole, 37.
Coleman, 81.
Collamore, XVII.–XVIII.

Collier, 52.
Colville, 42.
Comerford, 55.
Comnenus, XI.–XII.
Comstock, XIX.
Connaway, 87.
Conrad, 69.
Conrad of Rhenish France and his male line to Emperor Henry IV., X.–XII.
Convers or Converse, 84.
Coolidge, 15.
Corbin, 49.
Courtenay, XIV.
Coyle, 70.
Crawford, 63, XIX.
Creigh, 56.
Crouch or Croutch, 85.
Cummins, 81.
Cunningham, 51.
Curtiss, XIX.
Dandridge, 30, 31, 65.
Daniel, 30.
Davenport, XIX.
Davidson, 67–68, 70, XIX.
Davis, XVI., XIX.
Dawson, 16, 30, 75, XVIII.
Dean, 62–63.
Deans, 32.
De la Ware, see La Warr.
Denis, 28.
Dent, 55.
Devin, XIX.
De Voe, 81.
Dickeson, 27, XVII.
Digges, 48.
Dixon, 65.
Dorland, 77.
Downs, 60.
Drew, 51.
Drury, 26.
Ducas, XI.
Dudly, 16, 37.
Dunbar, 75, 80.
Duncan, 69, 73.
Dunn, 19.
Eakin, 54.
Earhart, 76.
Earp, 78–79.
Eaton, 30, 65, XIX.
Eberhard of Friuli, Emperor Berenger I., Berenger II., Adalbert, and their descendants in Burgundy, 90, X.–XII.
Eccleston, 25.
Echyngham, 8–12, XIV.–XV.
Edgar, 55.

Index.   93

Edbert, Alfred the Great, and their male descendants, 4, 90, VIII.-XI.
Edwards, 50.
Elliott, 13.
Ellyson, 18.
Elrington, see Erlington.
Eltonhead, 87.
Erlington, XV.
Este, XIX.
Eu, Count of, 90.
Evidence for the longest lines of the Chart, 5-12.
Ewing, 61, 74.
Faran, 62.
Farson, 64.
Fauntleroy, 16.
Felgate, 28.
Fenes or Ficnnes or Fenlis, 90.
Findlay, 54, 58, 61, 62, 64, 68-69.
Finley, 57.
Fisher, 51, 66.
Fitz Alan, 9, 10, XIII.-XIV.
Fitzhugh, 48, XIX.
FitzPiers, 90.
Flood, 48.
Foster, 27, 28, 29.
Franche Comté or Burgundy. See Eberhard.
Franconian Emperors. See Conrad of Rhenish France.
Freeman, 30.
French, 30.
Fritz, 68.
Fulton, 79.
Gadsden, 32.
Gamboa, XIII.
Garrett, 52.
Garretson, 32.
Gassaway, 62.
Gay, 61.
Ghibbeline. See Hohenstaufen.
Giberson, 81.
Gibson, 66.
Giesy, 63.
Gill, 19.
Gilliam, 52.
Giron, XIII.
Glyn, 87.
Goldston, XVI.
Gooch, 17.
Goodall, XVI.
Gordon, 48.
Graham, 57, 61.
Griffith, 62, XIX.
Grubb, 56, 64, 66.

Grymes, 14, 36, 49, 50.
Hack, 30.
Hage, 53.
Hall, 61.
Halys, XIV.
Hamilton, 55.
Hamm, 60.
Handy, 69.
Harleston, 8, XV.
Harman, 59, 60.
Haro, 6, XII.-XIII.
Harris, 65.
Harrison, 13-16, 30, 35, 36, 41-52, 55, 65, 77, 81, 88, XVII.-XIX.
Hawxhurst, 63.
Heneage, 25, 26.
Hendryx, XIX.
Henry the Fowler and his family, X.
Heth, 51.
Hewitt, 78.
Higginson, 35, XVII.
Hill, 14, 75, 81.
Hinde or Hind, 18, 19.
Hobson, 39, XVII.
Hohenstaufen, Dukes of Swabia, and Emperors, X.-XIII.
Honywood, 23-26, 29.
Hoo, 9.
Hopkins, 51.
Horton, 66, 85, 86.
Howell, XIX.
Hoyt, 80.
Huffman, 81.
Hunt, XIX.
Hunton, 54.
Hurle, 27, 39.
Huston, 65, 66.
Iden, 83.
Ingle, 33.
Inglis, 19.
Irvine, 63.
Irving, 51.
Irwin, 3, 53-66, 68, 77, XVIII.-XIX.
Italian line. See Eberhard.
Jack, 80.
Jeffries, 33.
Jenkins, XIX.
Johnson, 84, XIX.
Johnston, 63, 78-79.
Jones, 60.
Kay, 66.
Keesey, 59.
Kendall, 16.
Kennedy, 59, XIX.
Kent, 61.

Kersey, 46.
King, 19, 68, XVII., XIX.
Kingsmill, 22.
Kirkpatrick, 78.
Knivett or Knyvet, 10.
Krauth, 63.
Kuhn, 74-75.
Kulp, 55.
Laird, 78.
Langrish, XVI.
Landon, 88, XVII.
Lash, 64.
La Warr, 11-12, XIV.-XV.
Lear, 31, 37.
Legitimacy, 4-5.
Lee, 14, 16, 49, 56.
Lewis, 16, 17, 32, 33, XIX.
Lewkenore, 9.
Lightfoot, 17.
Lindsay, 42.
Linton, 69.
Lippincott, 55.
Littlejohn, 72.
Litton, XVI.
Lothrop, 63.
Louis d'Outremer, 5, X.
Ludlow, 5-6, 87, 88-89, XV.-XVII.
Ludwell, 35, 48-50, XVII.
Luttrell, 7, 8, XIV.-XV.
Lyddal or Liddell, 25, 26, 27.
Lyel, 73.
Lyons, 31.
Lytle, XIX.
McCarty, 31, XIX.
McClelland, 54-55, 64, 80.
McClung, 82, XIX.
McConnell, 53.
McDowell, 53, 54, 67-71, XVIII.
McFarland, 70.
McGahey, 56.
McGee, XIX.
McGonigal, 60.
McIntyre, 75, XIX.
McKee, XIX.
Mackenzie, 52, 59.
McKim, 51.
McKnight, 76.
McLandburg, 74.
McLaughlin, 68.
Maclay, 66, 68-69.
McNeeley, 82.
Magaw, 70.
Magill, 77.
Maitland, 52.
Maltravers, 9, 10, XIV.

Manfield, 25.
Manny, XIV.
Maris, 70.
Marny, 10.
Marott, 19, 21.
Marsh, 24.
Marshall, 36.
Martin, 70.
Maxwell, 68, 70.
Melchor, XIX.
Merewether, 16.
Merovingians. *See* Clovis.
Miller, 78.
Mills, 33.
Mitchell, 33.
Montgomery, 56.
Moore, 15, 27, XV.
More, 27.
Morgan, XIX.
Morris, 59, XIX.
Morrow, 74.
Morton, 58.
Moseley, 30.
Moss, 18, 19, 20.
Mowbray, 5, 11-12, XIV.
Murphy, 68.
Navarre. *See* Clovis.
Neal, XIX.
Neame, 84.
Neff, 70.
Nelson, 18, 37, 70.
Nesbith, 53.
Newall or Newell, 60, 67.
Newcomer, 66.
Newsum, 30,
Nicholas, 14, 36.
Nickels, XIX.
Noland, 15.
Norwood, 28, 29.
Nutting, 21.
Ogden, XIX.
Ogelsby, 59.
O'Neill, 75.
Osborne, 52.
Oxenbridge, 24.
Page, 14, 15, 36, 37, 51.
Painter, 75.
Paradise, 50.
Park, 80.
Parke, 35.
Parker, 59.
Patterson, 76.
Paull, 53.
Peachy, 18.
Peake, 26.

Pease, XIX.
Peck, 23, 25.
Percival, 73, XVIII.
Peterson, 52.
Phipps, XIX.
Pike, XIX.
Pile, 89, XVI.
Piper, 54, 71.
Plantagenet, 4, 12, 90, XII.-XIV.
Plummer, XIX.
Polk, 56, 64.
Porter, 53, 72-73, XVIII.
Postles, 60.
Potter, 82.
Poulton, 25.
Power, 34.
Powers, 19.
Presidents of U. S., 3, 21, 74, XIX.
Prothero, 80.
Provence, Count of, 12, 90, XIII.
Quaplad, 22.
Ramsay. See Ramsey.
Ramsey, 3, 57, 62, 64, 72-82, XVIII.-XIX.
Randolph, 14, 15, 40, 50, 51.
Raney, XIX.
Rawlins, XVI.
Reeder, 82.
Reeves, 63.
Reynolds, 60, 67, XIX.
Rice, 64.
Richardson, 77.
Riddell, 76-77.
Rigdon, 75.
Ringwood, XV.
Roberts, XIX.
Robertson, 79.
Robinson, 15, 19, 20, 75, 79.
Rogers, XIX.
Roper, 27.
Rose, XVII.
Rowan, 56.
Ruffin, 32, 52.
Russell, 19, 51.
Rymer, XV.
St. Clair, XVIII.
St. Leger, 88.
St. Nicholas, 25.
Saunders, XIX.
Saxon Kings in England. See Egbert.
Sayre, 32.
Schafer, XIX.
Schluter, 20.
Schreiner, 78.
Scott, 27, 29, 75, 88, XIX.
Scottish Kings, 90, XI.

Segrave, 11, XIV.
Selden, 19, 20.
Semple, 75.
Sheaff or Sheff, 25, 35.
Sheets, XIX.
Sheldon, 18, 21.
Sheriff, 23-24.
Sherley, 88.
Sherry. See Sheriff.
Shields, 21.
Shippen, 49.
Short, XIX.
Shunk, 59-60.
Sibley, 84.
Sidway, 46, 47, XVII.
Singleton, XIX.
Sloo, 61, 68.
Smith, 18, 22-26, 36, 51, 54, 56, 60, 62-64, 68, 69, 71, 79-80, XVII.
Soto-Mayor, XIII.
Souter, XIX.
Speer, 74-76.
Spicer, 78.
Stackhouse, 68.
Stith, 30, 31.
Storch, XIX.
Stratton, 7-8, XV., XIX.
Streeche, XIV.
Stringer, 47.
Suliard, 8.
Sumwault, 65.
Sutherland, 81-82, XIX.
Symmes, 83-84, 86, XVI.-XIX.
Tabb, 20.
Talbott, XIX.
Tasker, 17.
Tayloe, 14, 15, 22.
Taylor, 39, 51, 76, XVII., XIX.
Thacker, 38.
Theobald, 32.
Thompson, 13.
Thorley, 12, XV.
Thornton, 31, 48, XIX.
Tittle, 68.
Torrence, 68-69.
Torrey, XVII.
Turberville, 49.
Turner, 80, 81.
Tuthill, 85-86, XVI.-XVIII.
Tyler, 21.
Valois, Count of, XI.
Van Bibber, 32.
Van Lear, 55, 57-58.
Vaughn, XIX.
Vaulx or Vaux, 34.

Vause. *See* Vaulx.
Velasco, XIII.
Vere, XIV.
Vinal, XVII.
Wainwright, 76.
Wakelyn, 89.
Walcott, 66.
Walke, 18.
Walker, 14.
Warder, 55-56.
Ware, 77.
Warren, *Earls*, 90, XII.
Warner, 81.
Washington, 31, 33, 89.
Waters. *See* Atwater.
Watkins, 20.
Watts, 20.
Waugh, 72.
Wells, 85.
West, 11, 18, XIV.-XV., XIX.
Weston, 25.
Westwood, 18, 20.
Wheeler, 43.
White, 70.
Whitehill, 69.
Whiteman, 61, 65, XIX.

Wilkie, 73.
Wilkinson, 23.
Willetts, 60.
William the Conqueror and near descendants, 5, XI.-XII.
Willis, 36, XVII., XIX.
Willoughby, 89.
Wills, 27, 39, 40, 51.
Willson, XIX.
Wilson, 56, 74, 80, XIX.
Windsor *or* Wyndesor, 6-7, 12, XV.-XVI.
Wingate, 34, 35, XVII.
Winger, 56.
Withers, 52.
Wodford, 24.
Woodington, 34.
Woodward, 24-26, 79.
Woolmer, 85.
Work, 63, 80.
Wormeley, 13, 15, 37, 87, XVIII.
Wright,
Wyche, 7.
Wyeth, 59.
Young, 48, 62-63, 74, XIX.
Youngs, 85.
Zavallos, XIV.

ADDENDA TO ANCESTRY OF BENJ. HARRISON, PAGE 16.

Priscilla Churchill who m. Lewis, i.e. Col. John Lewis, by whom she probably left no issue, had previously m. " King" Carter's son, Robert of Nomini, who d. May, 1732, by whom she had "Councillor" Robert Carter and Elizabeth Carter, who m —— Willis.

PAGES 51 AND 52.

The name of Mayor Harrison's father was the same as his. Susanna Isham Harrison m. Rev. Samuel Blain, not Blaine.

ROBERT HARRISON, bro. of Signer, left issue:

Collier, of "Kittewan," Charles City Co., d. Nov., 1809, m., 1st, Christiana, née Shields, widow of —— Minge, and formerly of R. B. Armistead (p. 21), and, 2nd, Beersheba Bryant, and left by 1st wife: Eliz. Collier, b. in 1790, m. B. C. Harrison, grandson of the Signer (her issue to appear in Leach's work on the Signers), and Collier left by 2nd wife:

Robert Carter, of "Kittewan," m. Nancy Y. D., dau. of Joshua Poythress, issue: Jane Angus, d. unm., Robert Collier (d. at Elizabeth, N. J., in 1888, m. Jane DeHart Randolph of Va., issue, with 3 d. y.: Randolph Poythress of Elizabeth, N. J., and Clarence Howard of Fredericksburg, Va.), and Maitland, d. y.,

Braxton, of "Farmer's Rest," m. Camilla A. M. Johnson, issue: Mary, d. y., Adelaide (m. Lyttleton Royster, issue: Oceana H., Thos. H.,—dec'd, m. Lizzie Tilghman, née Camp, left: Thos. H.,—John B., and Annie S.), Oceana, d. y., Thomas P., unm., and Nannie B. (dec'd, m. John P. Tabb, left issue: J. Harrison, Robt. C., Braxton H., and Nannie P.),

Braxton, of "Farmer's Rest," d. s. p. in 1809.

HENRY HARRISON, who is 4th in John Herbert Peterson's list of the sons which Benj. Harrison left by his wife Miss Carter, lived at Hunting Quarter on Nottaway River, Sussex Co., d. before Oct. 28, 1775, m. ——, dau. of Cyril (?) Avery, and left, all minors at their father's death:

Henry, who m. Polly Cocke, and left: Henry John (last of "Hunting Quarter," d. s. p., m. two sisters, Mrs. Bland and Mrs. Wood) and Mary Rebecca, m. John M. Walker, M.D., and d. at birth of her only child, John Harrison Walker, who m. Louisa Cargill, and had, with 2 d. y.: Henry H. (Gen. C. S. A., m. Mary S. Mercer, issue: Mary M.,—m. Geo. Harrison of Brandon,—Louisa C., Henry H., Hugh Mercer, and Alice S.), Mary H., d. unm., Wm. W. (of Montgomery, Ala., m. Anna Shackelford, issue: Marianna,—m. —— Thompson,—Wm. W.,—m. —— Thompson,—Virginia, and Lucy P.), Geo. B., d. unm., Hugh B. (dec'd, m. Bettie Dodson, issue 2 d. y.), Louisa C. (m. T. S. McCall, no issue), Andrew S. (of N. Y.), and Robert Pegram (dec'd, m. Emma Smith, issue: Emma),

Elizabeth Randolph, d. Nov. 19, 1824, m. Nov. 13, 1789, (2nd w. of) Lewis Burwell of "Stoneland," Col. in the Revolution, who d. July 2, 1800, and they had:

Henry Harrison Burwell, b. Dec. 23, 1790, d. s. p. Jany. 3, 1815, m. Catharine Buford,
Peyton Randolph Burwell, b. July 29, 1792, m. Jane Seawell, issue: Eliz. Frances, d. inf. at burning of "Stoneland," Henry Harrison, d. unm., Nancy Ravenscroft (d. s. p., m. John J. Coleman), Jane Christian (m. Melancthon Read, issue: John L., Melancthon, Jane Christian, dec'd, Lucy, Panthea, Henry H., and P. Randolph), Selina Skipwith (m. Henry Tucker, issue: Henry Williamson,—m. Louisa Nelson,—Jane, Lewellyn, Eliz. Frances, and John Murray), Peyton Randolph, d. unm., Elizabeth H. (m. Wm. T. F. McCargo, issue: Selina C.,—m. Wm. B. Sherwood,—P. Randolph,—m. Ida Hodges,—Henry H.,—m. Mary A. Morrissey,—Emerson E.,—m. Clara Boone,—and Maria Hepburn, d. unm.), John Lewis (m. Nannie Womack, issue: Lula,—m. Cardoza), Mary Armistead (m. Wm. C. Boswell of Balt., issue: Nancy R., Thos.,—m. Sallie Brown,—John Lewis, Wm. C., Henry H., Lucy Burwell, and Mary A.), Fannie Courtney (m., 1st, George Hayes, and had: Edward, d. unm., and she m., 2nd, David Gayle, and had: Thomas), and Maria Hepburn (m. Darius Coleman, issue: John Randolph, Selina Skipwith, and Henry Harrison),

Jean Blair Burwell, b. Feb. 22, 1794, d. s. p., m. Wm. Eaton,
Martha Christian Burwell, b. Oct. 5, 1795, m., 1st, Chas. Grandison Feild, and, 2nd, (2nd w. of) his cousin John S. Feild, her children by whom d. inf., but she had by 1st husband: Mary E. (dec'd, m., 1st, Robt. Redd, M.D., and, 2nd, John B. Scott, and had, surname Scott: Charles, unm., Henry Harrison,—m. —— ——,—and Wm.), Thomas, d. unm., and Grandison (m. Catharine Reid, issue: Cordelia,—m. —— Shepherd,—Grandison, Thomas, Henry H., Catharine, Martha, and perhaps others),

i

Anne Carter, d. 1814, m. Nov. 26, 1788, Walter Cocke, and had:
    Walter Travis Cocke, m. Susan V. Coupland, granddau. of Benj. Harrison the Signer,
    Harrison Henry Cocke, b. May 10, 1794, captain U. S. N., resigned in 1861, d. Oct. 10, 1873, m., 1st, Elizabeth Ruffin, and, 2nd, Emily Banister, and had by 1st wife: Rebecca (m. Leonard Henley, M.D., issue: Leonard and Elizabeth), Tarifa (m. W. A. Witherspoon, issue: Harrison H., Charles D., Sally, and Wm. Alfred), Eliza, unm., and Juliana, unm., and by 2nd wife: Mary Munro (m. 1889 Walter Buck Richards of Mo. School of Mines, issue: Harrison Henry and James Neville), and Anne Harrison (m. George Mason, issue: Emily B. and John Blair),
    Martha Cocke, m. William A. Harrison, gr'dson of the Signer,
    Eliza Cocke, d. s. p., m. John Ponsonby.

NATHANIEL HARRISON, called "the 5th son" by Capt. H. H. Cocke, evidently not taking into account those who died young, was born, Sep. 30, 1742, according to the family record prepared by Nathaniel's son Edmund, and d. Dec. 24, 1782, m., 1st, Oct. 11, 1760, Mary Ruffin, b. June 5, 1739 (O. S.), d. Sep. 10, 1767, dau. of Edmund Ruffin, of Prince George Co., and, 2nd, Mch. 12, 1768, Anne Gilliam, d. April, 1781,

Issue by 1st wife:
    Anne, d. 1782, m. John Shore, M.D., issue: one son, d. unm.,
    Lucy, b. July 5, 1763, d. s. p. 1780, m., 1780, John Stith,
    Edmund, b. Dec. 12, 1764, of "The Oaks," Amelia Co., Va., d. Feb. 4, 1826, m., 1st, Mary Murray, who d. Jany. 18, 1804, and, 2nd, Nov. 22, 1806, Martha Wayles Skipwith, b. April, 1786, dau. of Henry Skipwith, issue by 1st wife: Edmund, d. y., and others d. inf., and by 2nd wife, with Anne Wayles, Helen Skipwith, and Octavia, who all d. y.:
        Wm. Henry, b. May 15, 1810, of "the Wigwam," Princ. of Amelia Acad., d. Dec. 23, 1881, m. in 1835 Lucy Ann Powers, who d. Oct. 29, 1881, and had, with 4 d. y.:
            Edmund, Prof. in Richmond College, m. Kate Steger, issue: Jane (m. C. H. Chalkley, M.D.), Lelia S. (m. Howard D. Hoge, issue: Edmund Harrison, Katie, Annie, and Howard D.), Kate, Lucy, Wm. Henry, John Steger, Edmund, and Roger Wayles,
            John Hartwell, of "the Wigwam," Amelia Co., m. Anna M. Carrington, issue, with 4 d. y.: I. Carrington, Sarah E., Joseph H., Robert C., Fred. Nash, and James Davis,
            Alice Wayles, m. Lewis H. Blair, issue, with 2 d. y.: Wm. Harrison, Walter D., Lewis H., Donald, and Lelia S.,
        Lelia Skipwith, unm.,
        Lucy Ashton, m. Chas. J. Faulkner, of Boydton, Va., issue, with 1 d. y.: Wm. Harrison, Thomas G., Chas. J., Sarah Alice, Lelia S., and Donald McK.,
        James Pinckney, lawyer in Danville, Va., m., 1st, Mary Jane Davis, and, 2nd, Caroline Rivers Douthat, widow (dau. of William M. Harrison, and granddau. of Thos. R. Harrison and Eliza Cunningham, p. 51 of ANCESTRY), issue by 1st w.: Lucy Landon and Donald Skipwith, and by 2nd w.: Carrie Rivers and Wm. Mortimer,
        Fanny Ballard, m. J. Hoyes Panton of Guelph, Canada, issue: Harrison Douglas, Donald McKenzie, d. unm.,
    Nathaniel, b. Dec. 23, 1812, d. about 1870, m. Mary Erskine, and had:
        Mary Randolph Skipwith, dec'd, m. —— Koch, and had issue,
    Lelia Skipwith, d. Feb. 17, 1868, m. Rev. Pike Powers, and had, besides Edm. H. and Lucy Ashton, both d. inf.:
        Alice Wayles Powers, d. s. p., m. John Baker Thompson,
        Anna Harrison Powers, unm.,
        Martha Skipwith Powers, m. Rev. Wm. H. Meade, and has, with 3 d. inf.: Alice W. (m. Robert Watson Prince, and had: Robert Watson, Patty Powers, and Wm. Meade), Harriotte Lee (m. James Berry Botts, and had: Wm. Meade), Anna P., Philip Randolph, and Pike Powers,
        Lelia Wayles Powers, m. W. Stuart Symington of Baltimore, and had: Lelia S. (m. John B. Goode, issue: Lelia Stuart, John B., and Clare Randolph), Thomas Harrison, Wm. Stuart, Powers, John Fife, Edmund Harrison, Donald Leith, and Charles Julian,
        Edmonia Carter Powers, m. George A. Barksdale, no issue,
        William Henry Harrison Powers (Rev.), m. Louise Sheffey, and had: Lelia Harrison, Louise Coles, Margaret Preston, Hugh White Sheffey, Muriel Skipwith, Douglas Harrison, and Donald Wayles,

Fanny Cary Powers, unm.,
Sally Carter, b. Aug. 18, 1816, d. s. p., m. W. D. Clark,
Donald McKenzie, b. Aug. 3, 1818, of Columbus, O., d. May 10, 1872, m. Dec. 30, 1850, Mary Jane Trabue, issue, with 1 d. y.: Edmund (of Columbus), Fanny Ann, Macon McK. (m. Anna Sommers, issue, with 1 d. y.: Anna May, Carl, Herbert, and Stanley), Eliz. Randolph, Patsy S., Mary Jane, Wm. Henry (m. Priscilla Long), and Benj.,
Septimia, b. Nov. 22, 1821, d. unm.,

Mary, b. Dec. 21, 1766, m. John Gilliam, her stepmother's nephew, and had:
- Mary Ruffin Gilliam, m. John Dunlop of Scotland, and had, with one d. inf., and John G., d. y., surname Dunlop:
   - James, m. Isabella L. Maitland, his mother's cousin, issue, with Mary C., d. y.: Susan Eliz. (m. Rev. A. F. Freeman, only issue: Frances Ann, m. Wm. Caruthers, and has Wm. F., Jas. M., Eliza S., and Frances Eliz. Caruthers), John (lawyer in Richmond, m. Mary Mildred Maury), Rob't Maitland (m. Eliza S. Gilliam, issue: Eliza S.), Colin McK., d. unm., Jas. (m. Lucy G. Kerr, issue: Jas. Kerr and Eliza Critcher), Donald McK. (of Balt., m. Mildred C. Lewis, issue: Jas., Rosa Isabelle, and Minna L.), Sarah H., unm., Marion L. M. (m. H. H. Baker of New Orleans, issue: Jas. M., J. Dunlop, and Colin McK.), Isabella M. (m. W. F. Spotswood, issue: Dandridge, Isabella M., Alex., Jas. D., Wm. F., Catharine F., Colin D., and Martha B. D.), Martha B., d. unm., and Catharine Mary, unm.,
- Donald McKenzie, d. s. p., m. Eliza Swinton of England,
- Marion, d. unm.,
- Mary Elizabeth, d. unm.,
- Jane Henry Gilliam, m. Wm. Baird, and had, with 3 d. y., surname Baird:
   - Mary H., m. Thos. P. Atkinson, M.D., issue: Agnes P. (m., 1st, Wm. Price, and had: Sally, and, 2nd, Benj. M. Jones, and had issue),
   - John, m. Mary Bolling, issue: Wm., d. unm.,
   - William (M.D.), m. Margt. Reid, issue: Wm. Westmore (m. Fannie Henderson, issue: Thos. Henderson and Leila), Thomas, Jane Ann, Virginia (m. Warren Brookes), and Algernon,
   - Henry Ruffin, m. Nannie Pleasants, issue: Jane G., Agnes P. (m. Chambliss, issue: Roger A.), Mary H. (m. Geo. C. Cabell, issue: Sallie,—m. Leonidas Lewis,—Nannie B.,—m. H. Wooding,—Benj., M.D., unm., Geo.,—m. Miss Gravely,—and Algernon), Roger, d. y., Eliz. W. (m. F. Thweatt), Henry R., d. unm., Nannie P., unm., Wm. Field (m. Louisa Jones), Eliza C. (m. T. A. Baird), and Ida B., d. unm.,
   - Nath'l H., m., 1st, Nancy B. Atkinson, and, 2nd, her cousin Agnes P. Atkinson, issue by 1st w.: Jno. Atkinson (m. Marie Reid), Jas. D. (m. Louisa Dickens), Wm. Gilliam (m. Eliz. Morton), Donald McK. (m. Pattie Edmunds), Mary Ann (m. J. Scott, M.D.), Anna (m. Edward Powell), Nath'l H. (m. Eliz. Holcomb), Thos. Atkinson (m. Eliza C. Baird, above), and by 2nd w.: Robert A.,
- Benj. Rice, m. Sarah Rowzie, issue: Edward R. (m. Jennie Barron) and Wm.,
- Thos. A., m. Lucy Perry, issue: Wm., Robert Perry, and Sarah,

Issue by 2nd wife:
Benjamin, m. a widow née Turnbull, and had:
- Nathaniel, M.D., of Puddledock, m., 1st, Mary Dandridge Minge, and, 2nd, Marg't Cargill, Issue by 1st wife:
   - Frances L., d. s. p., m. John P. Roberts,
   - Anne, of Petersburgh, unm.,
   - Benjamin, of Petersburgh, m. Jane Smith, issue: Anne, Nathaniel, and Mary G.,
   - Mary D., m. John P. May, issue, surname May: Nathaniel H. (m. Margaret King, issue: Mary D., Rosanna L., Margaret F., John P., and Wm. J.), David, Maria (m. P. Breeden, issue, surname Breeden, with 2 d. y.: Powhatan, Blanche, Wm., Edward, and Maria May), Wm. J., Anne H., d. inf., John F. (M.D., of Waverly, Va., m. Susie J. Warren, issue: Mary W., Susie J., and Evelyn), and Chas. Edw.,
   - Elizabeth, dec'd, m. Edward R. Turnbull, issue, surname Turnbull: Robert (lawyer at Lawrenceville, Va., m. Mary Harrison, issue: Edward R., Robt., Geo. H., Sallie W., Walter, Nath'l, Chas. D., Irby, Ellen A., and Benj. H.), Mary M. (m., 1st, Yelverton Tabb, and, 2nd, John Patterson, issue, surname Tabb: Eliz., Bertrand, Anne H., Yelverton, and Sarah Jane, and issue, surname Patterson: Mary), Eliz.,

d. unm., Nath'l H., d. unm., Edward Randolph (M.D., m. Daisey Barnes), Anne H. (m. Chas. O. Wheler, issue: Edward, Sadie, and Fannie), Sarah Jane (m. Irby Hardy), and Frances Lucy, unm.,

Sarah Jane, d. s. p., m. said Edward R. Turnbull,

Issue by 2nd wife:

Edmund, dec'd, m. Mary Steel, and had: Mary S., unm.,

Elizabeth, b. Aug. 31, 1770, d. s. p., m. —— Brown,

Nathaniel, b. Apr. 12, 1773, of Amelia Co., d. unm.,

Sallie Carter, b. July 10, 1775, d. s. p., m. Donald McKenzie,

Jane Pleasants, twin with Sallie C., m. John Osborne, and had:

John Harrison Osborne, d. unm.,

Charles Francis Osborne, m. Mary Field Gilliam, and had:

John Dunlop Osborne, d. unm.,

Charles Francis Osborne, m. Mary, dau. of Rev. Martin P. Parks, and left: Charles Francis (Asst. Prof. at Cornell Univ., m. Lucy Hutchinson),

Mary Jane Osborne, unm.,

James Gilliam Osborne, m. Alice, dau. of Rev. R. Terry, and left: Alice Harrison and Mary Gilliam,

Anne Eliza Osborne, m. Charles E. Hunt, issue: Mary Field, Charles Edwin, Francis Osborne, Cora Barksdale, Anne Eliza, Edith Read, and Eleanore Harrison,

Nathaniel Montgomery McKenzie Osborne, M.D., d. s. p., m., 1st, Mary Edloe, and, 2nd, Sarah McKenzie Maitland, his cousin,

Pleasants Carter Osborne, m. Adalina Stainback, and had:

Carter Stainback Osborne,

Sarah Jane Osborne, m. Wm. Willson, issue: Adalina Osborne (m. James H. McClevy, issue: Wm. Willson),

Nathaniel Montgomery Osborne, of Norfolk, m. Marion Meade, and has: Richard Kidder Meade, Nathaniel Montgomery, and Julien,

Caroline Pleasants Osborne,

Edmund Harrison Osborne, m. Sarah Cabaniss, and had:

Robert Cryer Osborne, m. Lucy Frances Dunn, and has: Sarah Cabaniss, Page Bragg, Joseph Dunn, and Mary Minton,

Jane Pleasants Harrison Osborne, m. W. Gordon McCabe, issue: Edmund Osborne, William Gordon, and Edward Raynesford Warner,

Elizabeth Minerva Osborne, m. John Rice Patterson, issue: Edmund Harrison (m. Susan Meade Nichols, issue: John R.) and Betty O. (m. Wm. A. Bragg),

John Dunlop Osborne, of Louisville, m. Harriet Graves, and had, with 1 d. y.:

William Graves Osborne, m. Foster Phillips, issue: Wm. Graves,

Jane Mary Osborne, m. James Cheston Worthington, Surgeon, U. S. A., and has Hallie and Mary Murray,

Hallie H. Osborne, m. John Bolling Bland, and has: John Osborne and Emily G.,

Sallie Osborne, unm.,

John, d. y. at college,

Susannah Boyd, d. July 6, 1812, m. Dec. 26, 1795, (1st w. of) Robert Maitland, of Petersburgh, Va., afterwards of Norfolk, son of David Maitland, of Scotland, and had, besides those who d. inf.:

Anne Mary Maitland, m. Thomas P. Devereux, of N. Car., issue: Susan Harrison, unm.,

Jane Catharine Maitland, d. s. p., m. Augustus F. Van Cortlandt,

Sarah McKenzie Maitland, d. s. p., m. her cousin, N. M. M. Osborne,

Martha Carter Maitland, d. unm.,

William Currie Maitland, b. Jany. 5, 1808, d. Aug. 16, 1882, m. Charlotte A. Ellison, issue: Mary Ellison, unm., Robert (m. Elizabeth Sullivan Lee, no issue), and Martha Carter (m. James Lord Bishop, of New York, issue: Mary Charlotte, Maitland Lathrop, and Merrill),

Isabella Lenox Maitland, m. James Dunlop, before mentioned.

CHARLES HARRISON, of the Revolutionary army, probably twin with Nathaniel, is said in Family Sketch by Charles's son-in-law Peterson to have been the youngest son, and not quite 19 at marriage, while the bride had just completed her 16th year, which would make 1761 the year of marriage, m. Mary Herbert Claiborne, d. July 25, 1775, dau. of Augustine and Mary (née Herbert) Claiborne, and had, besides Augustine, d. inf.:

Charles, in U. S. Army, killed in duel, unm.,

Mary Herbert, b. "Berkeley," Sep. 11, 1766, d. in Prince George Co., Jany. 15, 1833, m. April 9, 1795, her first cousin, John Herbert Peterson, who d. Dec. 26, 1830, they had, with 2 d. y.:
  John Augustine Peterson, m., 1st, Virginia Ann, d. 1824, dau. of J. J. Thweatt, and, 2nd, Eliza, dau. of Richard Thweatt,
    Issue by 1st wife :
      John Augustine, m., 1st, Mary Epes, and, 2nd, Clara Cole, widow, issue by 1st w.; John A. (m. —— Smith), Harriet, and Mary (m. Ervin Barnes), and by 2nd w.: Virginia (m. J. T. Golden) and Weldon,
      Virginia Ann Thweatt, m. Nath'l Cocke, issue, with one d. y.: Mary H. (m. Rich. H. Smith), Jno. Jas. (lawyer in Petersburgh, m. Sarah Atwater), Sally C. (m. Clarence R. Hotton), Nannie Hayes (m. Alex. H. Smith), Virginia P. (m. Wm. Edw. Smith), Nath'l, Elizabeth, Thos., and Chas. H.,
    Issue by 2nd wife :
      Mary Frances, of Petersburgh, unm.,
      Richard Harrison, m. Ella Marks, issue: Ida (m. John Thomas), Rich'd (m. Jessie Meyers), Cornelia, Sallie, Ella (m. Richard Beamish), Herbert, and William,
      Cornelia, m. Armistead Plummer, issue : Mary (m. Sidney Green), Wm. (m. Virginia Edwards), John Peterson (m. Nannie Strachan), Susan (m. S. N. Urquhart), Edward (m. Ollie Smith), Ann T., Powhatan, Georgie (m. L. Smith), Armistead, Louisa (m. Kirk Scabery), Herbert, Frank, and Julia,
      Elizabeth, unm.,
  Lucy Ann Peterson, d. s. p., in Oct., 1828, m. Wm. H. Young,
  Maria Harrison Peterson, m. John Prentis, they removed to Kentucky in 1833, and afterwards to Spencer Co., Ind., and both d. of cholera in 1849, issue, with 3 d. y., surname Prentis:
    John Peterson, b. 1823, d. 1888, m. Margt. M. Morton, issue, with one d. y.: Margt. Hamlen (m. Geo. Stephens), George Peterson (m. Isabella Paine), and Luther Morton,
    Maria Louisa, of Evansville, Ind., m. Davis Lincoln Connor, killed in Union army in 1863, issue, with 2 d. y., surname Connor: Martin Harrison (m. Martha V. Gregory, issue : Jas. Harrison, Wm. Gregory, and Robt. Austin), James Peterson, and William A. (m. Mary Alice McGuinney, issue : Clarence Orville, Maria Olive, Arch'd Harrison, Robt. Peterson, Wm. Clyde, and Hazel Rosena),
    Thomas Augustine, d. unm., drowned in 1851,
    Lucy Harrison, m., 1st, Edwin M. Fenn, and, 2nd, Hardin P. Wood, issue, surname Fenn, with one d. inf.: Edwin Peterson (m. Louisa Little) and Sam'l Prentis (m. Sallie Rogers), and, surname Wood : Mazella Harrison and Ida Belle,
    Emily Rosena, d. 1876, m., 1st, Caswell Watts, and, 2nd, Robt. Porter, issue, surname Watts, with one d. y.: Elijah S. (m. Nannie R. Beatty), and, surname Porter: Chas. (m. Laura Arnold), Anna L. (m. Wm. Jones), Sallie (m. ——), Maria B. (m. Wm. Hargist), and Ella Rosena,
Anne Carter, m. Matthew Maury Claiborne, her cousin, and had, besides 2 d. y.:
  Matthew Maury Claiborne, 2nd Lieut. U. S. A. in 1814, afterwards of Baltimore, m. —— McKoon (?), widow, his cousin, whom he survived, issue: Mary, d. y. about 1832,
  Susan Carter Claiborne, m. Wm. Sumner, Major, and had: William and Sarah Anne Sumner, who removed from Baltimore to the West,
  Martha Anne Herbert Claiborne, m. Mch. 15, 1821, James B. Mannar, issue, with Charles H., d. y., surname Mannar :
    Almira, dec'd, m. Pierre Thomas, issue: Alphonse, Pierre E., and Martha,
    Louisiana, dec'd, m. Benj. Bowen, issue: Jas. Claiborne, John Oswald, and Sallie M. (m. A. Evans Wands),
    Virginia, m. Joshua A. Adams, issue: John Quincy,
    Claiborne Harrison, of N. Y., m., 1st, Feb. 22, 1861, Isabella Bryant Flack, and, 2nd, Nov., 1890, Frances E. A. Gutch, by whom no issue, issue by 1st wife, with 2 d. y.: Claiborne H. (m. Angelina R. Beall, issue d. y.),
    Estella, dec'd, m. Alex. B. Webber, issue : J. Claiborne and Estelle,
    Anne Claiborne, m. Aaron Clary, no issue,
    Emma, m. John Begnette, issue: Mollie Augusta (m. Josiah A. Kinsey), Wm., Eliz. (m. Henry Clary, issue : 3 children), John, James T., Chas. H., Jennie, and Nannie,

Mary Claiborne, m. John Richardson, no issue,
Martha A. H., m. Wm. Quarle Caldwell, issue, with 3 d. y.: Cora L. (m. Enoch M. Barker, issue: Cora L. and Ralph Caldwell) and Herbert Claiborne,
Maria Randolph Claiborne, b. Nov. 19, 1802, d. Aug. 8, 1839, m. Sep. 12, 1822, Thos. G. Gutch, of Bristol, England, who d. Nov. 2, 1868, issue, with Ann C., d. y.: Frances Eliz. Ann, m. (2nd w. of) Claiborne H. Mannar, above,
Charles Harrison Claiborne, m. Caroline E. Cloud, issue: Jesse Cloud, Ann Carter, Mary Elmira (d. s. p., m. Paul Crummer), Malvina Matilda, Caroline Elizabeth, and Julia Claiborne, who all d. s. p., besides
 Charles Harrison Claiborne, of Baltimore, the 5th child, m. Jane E. Cannon, of Spartanburg, S. C., issue: Frances Ellen (m. J. Rufus Cato, of Atlanta), Jane Eliz. (m. John Owen, of Atlanta, issue: Eva M.), Chas. H. (m. Cora N. Ludlum), Eva Cloud, and Margarette May,
Benjamin Henry, b. June 30, 1775, m. Eliz. Claiborne Butts, sister of D. C. Butts, below, and had 2 children, who both d. inf.,
Elizabeth Randolph, twin with B. H., m. Daniel Claiborne Butts, General, and had:
 Mary Harrison Butts, b. Sep. 12, 1796, m. Nov. 18, 1819, Jas. M. Davidson, of Richmond, issue, with James Montgomerie and Eloise Rebecca, who both d. y., and Agnes Maury and Chas. Harrison, who both d. unm.:
  William Butts Davidson,
  Washington LaFayette Davidson (Rev.), d. 1859, m. Julia V. McNeir, issue, with 2 d. y.: Julia Virginia (m. Jas. E. Ackroyd, of Phila., issue: Grace Davidson, Julia May, and Helen Hamilton),
  Mary Elizabeth Davidson, unm.,
  Virginia Emeline Davidson, unm.,
  Nora Fontaine Maury Davidson, unm.,
 John Butts, M.D., d. in Greene Co., Ala., Aug. 10, 1843, aged 44, m. Amanda, dau. of Person Turner of Greensville Co., Va., issue: John (M.D., m. Mary Knox, née Shelby, no issue), Mary Eloise Maury (m. D. N. Moody, Col., issue, with 3 d. y.: Mary E.), Edward S. (of Vicksburg, m., in 1886, Lucy McCutchen, issue: Evelyn Turner), Eliz. Randolph Harrison (m. Joel Willis, no issue), and Eva Turner (dec'd, m. Wm. Dashiell, issue: Edw. Butts, d. y.),
 Daniel Claiborne Butts, b. 1801, Capt., d. May 2, 1876, m., 1821, Ariadne Elmira Smith, and had:
  Amanda Butts, d. s. p. Aug. 21, 1891, m. Richard Baptist,
  Virginia LaFayette Butts, unm.,
  Marie Eloise Butts, m. Robert Dunlop of Petersburgh, issue: Agnes Aitkin (m. William H. Wight, of Baltimore, issue: Robert Dunlop), Robert (M.D., of Louisville, Ky.), Daniel B., and Marie Ariadne (m. Warner Moore, issue: Janie Marie and Warner),
  Augusta Chamberlayne Butts, dec'd, m. T. F. Scott, M.D., left issue: Walter, William Wingfield (m. Flora Gay), Ida (m. Edward Peebles of Petersburgh, and left Thomas and Edward), Ashton Lewis (M.D., of Wilmington, N. C.), and John Dodson, of N. Y.,
  Benjamin Harrison Butts, dec'd, m., 1st, Ophelia Clay, and, 2nd, Miss Miles, issue by 1st w.: Agnes D., d. unm. Nov. 20, 1877, Bettie Ophelia, and Marcellus Bell, and by 2nd w.: Evelyn, Nelson Patteson, dec'd, Juliette Amanda, Laura, Marie, Wm. Henry, and Benj. H.,
  Daniel Claiborne Butts, d. unm.,
  William Henry Harrison Butts, d. unm.,
  John A. Butts, m. Mary Ann Patton, issue: John A., d. y., and Florence Virginia,
  Ariadne Butts, m. Octavius Smith, issue: Ariadne C.,
  Richard Edward Butts, m. Saraphine Carpenter, issue: Daniel C. and Edward R.,
 Martha Elizabeth Butts, b. 1804, d. Baltimore, 1847, m. John Lakenan, Major, and had issue:
  Virginia Harrison Butts Lakenan, m. Charles Getzendanner, no issue,
  Louie Harrison Butts Lakenan, m. Chas. H. Cowman, now of Baltimore, issue, with 4 d. y.: Henry Snowden, Helen May Randolph, and Louie Stewart Harrison,
Augustine Claiborne Butts, b. Nov. 17, 1806, Colonel, d. Aug. 15, 1870, m., 1st, Martha R. Stewart, d. 1832, and, 2nd, Mary E. Maclin, d. 1846, and, 3rd, Anna Maria Claiborne, his second cousin, d. 1863, and, 4th, Fannie J. Lundy, d. s. p. 1875,

Issue by 1st wife:
Josephine Martha Stewart Butts, unm ,
Issue by 2nd wife, besides five, who d. inf.:
Susan Maclin Butts, m. W. W. Guy of Memphis, issue: Hester Elizabeth (m. —— Swift) and Medora Augusta (m. —— Joyner),
Robert Emmet Butts, killed in battle, d. unm.,
Issue by 3rd wife:
Daniel Gregory Claiborne Butts (Rev.), of Mathews, Va., m. A. Emma Swann, issue: Mary C., Anna Maria Waller, Herbert Swann, Carrie Weldon, Emmet Dabney, and Emma Gregory,
Eloise Maury Butts, m. John T. Jackson of Ala., General, issue, with 1 d. y. and 2 d. unm.: Marion Henry, m. Penelope Jones, left: Emmett B. and Gay T. (m. Charlie Hall, issue: Luther and Charlie),
Laura Davidson, m., 1st, W. S. P. Hunt, and, 2nd, J. W. Fore, issue by 1st husband: W. Isabella (m. S. B. Jackson, Judge), and by 2nd husband: John P. J. (m. Lillie Farral, issue: Willie),
Rosa Virginia, m. Robt. S. Waddle, issue, with 3 d. y.: Elouisa M. B. (m. E. T. Elmer, issue: Robt. Jas., Mary V., Eugene T., and Willie Ramsey), Saidee Christian (m. W. M. Ramsey, below), and Robt. Emmett Augusta, unm.,
Norborne Herbert Tucker, m. three times, issue by 2nd w.: Eloise M., Norborne H., and Marion Henry, and by 3rd w.: Edgar,
Evelyn Fontaine, d. s. p., m., Charles Kimball,
Benj. Henry Harrison Butts, of Texas, d. s. p., m. Miss Lakenan,
Emma Cadwallader Butts, m., 1st, Wm. Thos. Harwell, and, 2nd, Launcelot V. Underwood,
Issue by 1st husband:
Ella Davidson Harwell, dec'd, m. John Milton Ramsey, left issue: Wm. Milton (of Meridian, Miss., m. his cousin, Saidee C. Waddle, and has: Wm. Milton) and Jas. Bascom (m. Lizzie Lonegan),
Laura Elizabeth Harwell, dec'd, m. Thos. Wilson Myers, left issue: Lula (dec'd, m. Lilburn Dozier, left 2 children) and Charles,
William Thomas Harwell, killed in battle May 8, 1864, d. unm.,
James Daniel Harwell, of Meridian, Miss., m., 1st, Annie Leah Smith, and, 2nd, Minnie Minge Friend, by whom no issue, issue by first wife: James Maury, Florence Annie, Herbert Thomas, Wm. Minor, Mary Emma, Bettie Julia, and John Allen,
Issue by 2nd husband, with 2 d. y.:
Mary Emma Underwood, dec'd, m. Slater Dozier, and left issue: Merlyn,
Daniel Launcelot Underwood, dec'd, m. Mollie Mason, and left issue: Bessie.

PAGE 53.

The Ensign Archibald Irwin of the French and Indian War was evidently the Archibald who died in the winter of 1798-9, the name of his father being, not Archibald, but James. The latter's will, dated May 26, 1776, probat. Apr. 21, 1778, leaves to son Archibald the plantation adjoining that on which the testator resided, and mentions a wife Jean and the children as on p. 53, except that Mary is omitted, but son-in-law Wm. Nesbit is named, and instead of two married to McConnells, there were Elizabeth, wife of Aaron Torrens, formerly wife of Wm. McCune, and Margaret, wife of Thomas Patton.

PAGE 88.

The tombstone over "King" Carter's first wife, erected presumably by himself or his son, is decorated with two shields each bearing the Carter paternal arms (a chevron bet. 3 cartwheels) impaled. The female side of one shield bears 3 crosses crosslet, and is to be interpreted as representing the emigrant John Carter's mother or paternal grandmother. The female half of the other shield, a chevron bet. 3 heads, erased, of animals evidently martins (as borne by Ludlow), confirms the statement, first printed by Bp. Meade, apparently from records or tradition gathered by John Minor, that "King" Carter was the issue of the Ludlow marriage. Minor, who was great-great-grandson of "King" Carter and his 2nd wife, Betty, says that Betty's mother was a St. Leger. Betty's father came to Virginia, and his will identifies him with Thomas, son of Silvanus Landon, which Silvanus married, as his 2nd wife, the widow of St. Leger. Thomas may have married St. Leger's daughter.

www.ingramcontent.com/pod-product-compliance
Lightning Source LLC
Chambersburg PA
CBHW020145170426
43199CB00010B/901